TINKER *v.*
DES MOINES

Landmark Supreme Court Cases

TINKER *v.*
DES MOINES

THE RIGHT TO PROTEST IN SCHOOLS

by Marcia Amidon Lusted

Content Consultant
Gerald J. Thain
Professor of Law Emeritus
University of Wisconsin–Madison

CREDITS

Published by ABDO Publishing Company, PO Box 398166, Minneapolis, MN
55439. Copyright © 2013 by Abdo Consulting Group, Inc. International
copyrights reserved in all countries. No part of this book may be reproduced in
any form without written permission from the publisher. The Essential Library™
is a trademark and logo of ABDO Publishing Company.

Printed in the United States of America,
North Mankato, Minnesota
062012
092012

Editor: Melissa York
Series Designer: Emily Love

Library of Congress Cataloging-in-Publication Data
Lusted, Marcia Amidon
  Tinker v. Des Moines : the right to protest in schools / by Marcia Amidon
Lusted ; content consultant: Gerald Thain.
      p. cm. -- (Landmark Supreme Court cases)
  Includes bibliographical references.
  ISBN 978-1-61783-477-6
  1. Tinker, John Frederick--Trials, litigation, etc.--Juvenile literature. 2. Des
Moines Independent Community School District--Trials, litigation, etc.--
Juvenile literature. 3. High school students--Civil rights--United States--Juvenile
literature. 4. Freedom of speech--United States--Juvenile literature. 5. Vietnam
War, 1961-1975--Protest movements--Iowa--Des Moines--Juvenile literature. 6.
Trial and arbitral proceedings. I. Thain, Gerald J. II. Title. III. Title: Tinker v.
Des Moines. IV. Title: Tinker versus Des Moines.
  KF228.T56L87 2013
  342.7308'53--dc23
                              2012001280

Photo Credits
Bettmann/Corbis/AP Images, cover, 15, 37, 42, 127; Record Journal, Johnathon
Henninger/AP Images, 3, 139; Warren K. Leffler/Library of Congress, 10, 50;
Horst Faas/AP Images, 21; Library of Congress, 24; Robert W. Klein/AP Images,
28; AP Images, 32, 77, 98, 116, 118; Manfred Grimm/iStockphoto, 53; Ferd
Kaufman/AP Images, 56; Des Moines Register, 65, 95; Leonard Mccombe/Time
& Life Pictures/Getty Images, 72; Joel Carillet/iStockphoto, 87; Photograph
by Steve Petteway, Collection of the Supreme Court of the United States, 109;
Marion S. Trikosko/Library of Congress, 112; ZUMA Wire Service/Alamy, 138

Table of Contents

WHAT IS THE US SUPREME COURT?

The US Supreme Court, located in Washington DC, is the highest court in the United States and authorized to exist by the US Constitution. It consists of a chief justice and eight associate justices nominated by the president of the United States and approved by the US Senate. The justices are appointed to serve for life. A term of the court is from the first Monday in October to the first Monday in October the following year.

Each year, the justices are asked to consider more than 7,000 cases. They vote on which petitions they will grant. Four of the nine justices must vote in favor of granting a petition before a case moves forward. Currently, the justices decide between 100 and 150 cases per term.

The justices generally choose cases that address questions of state or federal laws or other constitutional questions they have not previously ruled on. The Supreme Court cannot simply declare a law unconstitutional; it must wait until someone appeals a lower court's ruling on the law.

HOW DOES THE APPEALS PROCESS WORK?

A case usually begins in a local court. For a case involving a federal law, this is usually a federal district court. For a case involving a state or local law, this is a local trial court.

If a defendant is found guilty in a criminal trial and believes the trial court made an error, that person may appeal the case to a higher court. The defendant, now called an appellant, files a brief that explains the error the trial court allegedly made and asks for the decision to be reversed.

An appellate court, or court of appeals, reviews the records of the lower court but does not look at other evidence or call witnesses. If the appeals court finds no errors were made, the appellant may go one step further and petition the US Supreme Court to review the case. A case ruled on in a state's highest court may be appealed to the US Supreme Court.

A Supreme Court decision is based on a majority vote. Occasionally one or more justices will abstain from a case, however, a majority vote by the remaining justices is still needed to overturn a lower-court ruling. What the US Supreme Court decides is final; there is no other court to which a person can appeal. In addition, these rulings set precedent for future rulings. Unless the circumstances are greatly changed, the Supreme Court makes rulings that are consistent with its past decisions. Only an amendment to the US Constitution can overturn a Supreme Court ruling.

Chapter 1

The Right to Protest

To many observers, it seemed the case would be an easy win for lawyer Dan Johnston. It seemed like a clear-cut case of a school board suspending students without sufficient cause, just for wearing black armbands to school to protest against the Vietnam War. Proving the school board had violated the students' right to free speech and free expression seemed as if it would be simple.

But after two years in the court system, the case came before the Eighth Circuit US **Court of Appeals**. The court issued a split decision on November 3, 1967. This outcome meant the opinion of the lower federal court—a ruling against the students and in favor of the school district—still stood. What had seemed like a simple case of students exercising their right to free speech would now have to be appealed to the US Supreme Court. But Johnston was not completely disappointed by the ruling of the court of appeals. A dream of many lawyers was arguing a case before the highest court in the country, and it looked as though Johnston was going to get his chance.

Christopher Eckhardt, one of the students who had been suspended, was also surprised. Years later he would comment,

> *I knew at the time that the US Supreme Court consisted of nine dudes in black robes who made decisions that affected the rest of the country. But never in my wildest dreams did I ever think we would end up in front of the Supreme Court.*[1]

A Two-Inch Piece of Cloth

It all began in 1965. War was raging in Vietnam, a country in Southeast Asia that was divided over communism. The United States was fighting the war

---

court of appeals—A federal court that hears cases appealed from the district courts in its circuit.

Many Vietnam War protests took place outside the White House.

to help defeat the Communist forces. Thousands of US soldiers had already died in the effort. Although Americans were shocked by the realities of the fighting they saw broadcast on their television news every night, many of those who opposed the spread of communism still supported the war. But a growing group of people, many from colleges and universities, opposed US involvement and firmly believed Americans did not belong in Vietnam. It was a time of protests, from demonstrations to burning draft cards. A man even covered himself with gasoline and set himself on fire to protest the killings in Vietnam.

During this time, several students in Des Moines, Iowa, decided to express their opinions about the Vietnam War—in particular, their disapproval of the loss of American lives and their belief in the need for a cease-fire—by wearing black armbands to school on December 16 and 17, 1965. During a meeting held at the Eckhardt home on December 11, a number of students agreed to wear the black armbands. The plan seemed like a small, peaceful way to express their opinions on the Vietnam War. But this small action would result in more than three years of school board controversy and court cases. As they went to school on that cold December 16 in Des Moines, John and Mary Beth Tinker and Christopher Eckhardt had no idea their actions would have such lasting repercussions in US **constitutional** law.

Many years later, Christopher would describe the day in 1965 when he arrived at Roosevelt High School. He was 15 years old, a sophomore, and he was about to

constitutional—In accordance with a constitution.

11

become the first person in the United States ever to be suspended from school for wearing a black armband. The Des Moines school district had a rule prohibiting anything that might create a disturbing situation in a school environment, and at a school board meeting only days before, this prohibition had been discussed and the specific act of wearing a black armband was included as a violation of this rule. Christopher's intention was to arrive at school and then turn himself in to the principal, having broken the school district rule as an act of **civil disobedience**. Christopher recalled:

> We walked quietly through the doors on the northeast side of the building, and up the stairs to my corner locker. . . . I took off my overcoat, and there for all the world to see, was my scarlet letter. Well, really it was just a two inch wide piece of black cloth I had safety pinned to my camel jacket.[2]

Two other Roosevelt High School students would also be suspended for wearing armbands that day: sophomore Christine Singer and senior Bruce Clark. Bruce met Christopher at school on December 16 and

---

civil disobedience—A refusal to obey the government or laws in order to protest government action.

CIVIL DISOBEDIENCE

Henry David Thoreau, an American author and philosopher, coined the term *civil disobedience* in 1848. After spending a night in jail for refusing to pay a poll tax, Thoreau wrote his famous essay titled "Civil Disobedience." He wrote, "Unjust laws exist; shall we be content to obey them, or shall we endeavor to amend them . . . ?"[3] Throughout US history, ordinary individuals have engaged in civil disobedience to protest unjust laws. During the mid-twentieth century, the civil rights movement used these tactics to improve rights for African Americans. Civil rights leaders, including Martin Luther King Jr., were famous for their acts of civil disobedience.

accompanied him to the principal's office. Singer wore her armband on the same day. All three students were suspended until after winter break. They were allowed to return immediately on the condition that they not wear their armbands again, but Christopher refused. Christine and Bruce decided to return to school without their armbands.

Meanwhile, at Harding Middle School, also in Des Moines, Mary Beth likewise went to school that day wearing a black armband. She was only 13 and in eighth grade. She did not intend to turn herself in to the school's principal but simply went to her classes as usual. During one class, she circulated a petition saying students should have the right to wear things such as armbands and crucifixes to school. No one seemed to pay much attention to her armband until her math class, when the teacher sent her to the principal's office. There, the girls' adviser for the school told her she had violated a school district rule, and the adviser had no choice but to suspend her. As Mary Beth remembers:

> I was sent home and I was really shocked that later that night the newspapers and the press came around and they were interested because I thought that you had to do something really important to be in the newspapers and I knew what we did was this really small thing.[4]

Mary Beth's brother John was 15 and a sophomore at North High School in Des Moines. He had not worn an armband on December 16. He felt the school administration should be given the opportunity to change its mind about banning armbands. But when his sister was sent home and the school board president referred to the armband issue as a trivial matter, John decided to wear an armband to his school the next day. When he got to school, he pinned the black armband onto his jacket. Several students commented on his

Mother Lorena Tinker, *left*, encouraged her children, including Paul, *center*, and Mary Beth, *right*, to form political opinions.

armband in a negative way, insulting him, and some warned him he was going to be suspended like his sister. A few students were supportive. John was not formally suspended. If he stopped wearing the armband, he was told he could return to school and there would be no negative effect on his grades or his school record. However, John refused to remove the armband, and he went home with his father.

The other participants who wore black armbands to school that month were Hope and Paul Tinker, younger siblings of John and Mary Beth. Their actions did not attract any unusual attention at their elementary school, and the teacher in Hope's class even turned the incident into a teaching moment.

The simple action of wearing an armband to school, carried out peacefully by these students without any aggressive behavior or verbal protests, seemed like something that would be handled by the schools' administrators and quickly forgotten. But there was a larger issue here about students' right to free speech, and it was not long before the incident moved beyond the schools.

The Controversy Spreads

By Friday, December 17, the armband issue had already attracted broader attention. The Tinker and Eckhardt families had requested the Iowa Civil Liberties Union (ICLU) look into the controversy to see if it was legal for the school district to prohibit students from wearing armbands. Craig Sawyer, who was an assistant professor at Drake Law School in Des Moines, announced that he had been asked by the ICLU to represent the suspended

THE AMERICAN CIVIL LIBERTIES UNION

The ICLU is affiliated with the American Civil Liberties Union (ACLU). The ACLU fights for the civil rights of Americans, even if the cause is unpopular. It was founded in 1920. Its staff and volunteer lawyers handle civil liberties cases across the country. The ACLU has been involved with many landmark cases in US history. It has represented unpopular groups with ideals the ACLU does not necessarily agree with, such as the American Nazis, showing the organization's unbiased defense of civil rights. For 90 years, the ACLU has been involved with more Supreme Court cases than any other private organization.

students at the next school board meeting. The ICLU released its own statement:

> In connection with the present prohibition against the wearing of black arm bands in the Des Moines Public Schools, the Iowa Civil Liberties Union expresses regret that students have been suspended for using what is otherwise a permissible means of expression. . . . It is hoped that the School Board will review the action of the school's administration and in so doing fully recognize and protect the students' right to freely express themselves, even though the subject matter is controversial or concerns an unpopular point of view.[5]

THE FIRST AMENDMENT

The armband controversy became a celebrated court case because of the charge that the school district violated the First Amendment rights of students, which include the right to free speech. The American Civil Liberties Union felt the right of the students to wear black armbands to express their opinions against the Vietnam War was included in free speech. The exact wording of the First Amendment is:

Congress shall make no law respecting an establishment of religion, or prohibiting the free exercise thereof; or abridging the freedom of speech, or of the press; or the right of the people peaceably to assemble, and to petition the Government for a redress of grievances.[7]

The Des Moines school board argued it was not trying to stifle free speech and said it did believe there was a place for discussing controversial ideas within the school. The board explained its fear that an action such as wearing an armband could be disruptive and even incite violence in the schools. Superintendent Dwight Davis said, "It's not that we don't think these students should have views and be willing to stand up for them. . . . You have to draw the line somewhere."[6] The school board president, Ora Niffenegger, was even clearer, saying he was "absolutely opposed to this type of demonstration within the confines of the school."[8]

From the small act of wearing a black armband to school, the incident blossomed into a debate whether students' constitutional rights to free speech and free expression stopped at the door of the school. Through the next three years of court cases, this question would be explored and argued again and again, and the case of *Tinker v. Des Moines* would become a landmark in **judicial** history. ~

judicial—Relating to justice or the courts.

Chapter 2

1965

*J*ust what were the circumstances that led
three students at small Midwestern schools to
protest? The United States in 1965 was a turbulent
place. There were struggles for African-American
civil rights and for equal rights for women. But many
believed the biggest issue affecting Americans was
the Vietnam War, which had been ramping up in the
tiny country in Southeast Asia since the late 1950s,
when the first US troops arrived. It was an issue that
generated protests all over the country and divided
people into those who supported the war and those
who did not.

The United States sent increasing numbers of troops to Vietnam through the 1950s and 1960s.

A Communist Threat?

The country of Vietnam had once been a colony of France, but after World War II (1939–1945) it became engulfed in a civil war. A dictator ruled the South Vietnamese, while the North Vietnamese were supported and armed by the Communist countries of China and the Soviet Union. In its purest form, communism was meant to eliminate the differences between the rich and poor by giving everyone in society an equal share, with everything owned by the state. However, communism in practice became a system under which a strong central government suppressed the rights of the people, often silencing those who spoke out against it. The system in practice clashed with the democratic system of the United States, and the threat of more Communist countries was seen as a threat to democracy everywhere. Many of the advisers to the US presidents during the years following World War II felt that allowing Vietnam to become a Communist country would lead to other countries in Southeast Asia becoming Communist as well. There was a pervasive fear that Communists would begin to take over more and more countries, endangering democratic countries. The US government wanted to establish democracy in as many places as possible, and it was willing to send US troops to Vietnam to fight against communism. As President Lyndon B. Johnson said in a speech on US policy in Vietnam in April 1965:

> " If I left [the war in Vietnam] and let the Communists take over South Vietnam, then I would be seen as a coward and my nation would be seen as an appeaser, and we would both find it impossible to accomplish anything for anybody anywhere on the entire globe."[2]
>
> —*PRESIDENT LYNDON B. JOHNSON, DESCRIBING THE EVENTS OF 1965 IN 1970*

> *Over this war and all Asia is another reality: the deepening shadow of communist China. . . . This is a regime which . . . is helping the forces of violence in almost every continent. The contest in Vietnam is part of a wider pattern of aggressive purposes. Why are these realities our concern? Why are we in South Vietnam? We are there because we have a promise to keep. Since 1954 every American president has offered support to the people of South Vietnam. . . . Over many years, we have made a national pledge to help South Vietnam defend its independence.[1]*

US soldiers were drafted to serve in Vietnam. The modern military draft system was established in 1940 for

The war in Vietnam escalated under President Johnson.

World War II by the creation of the Selective Service. It was a process of requiring young American men to serve in the military, especially when there were not enough volunteers to supply the military. Men were required to register for the draft and could be called into service. Only full-time college students or men with physical or mental disabilities were excused from serving. The age of men eligible for the draft has fluctuated over time. During the Vietnam War, men aged 18 to 26 had to register for the draft.

By 1965, more than 180,000 US troops were in Vietnam fighting against the North Vietnamese. And in that year alone, more than 1,800 US troops were killed in the war.[3] Many South Vietnamese soldiers and civilians were also being killed. These death tolls would

WAR DEATHS

The total number of deaths of US military personnel in the Vietnam War:

Air Force	2,584
Army	38,209
Coast Guard	7
Marine Corps	14,838
Navy	2,555
Total	58,193[4]

continue to climb, and by the end of the Vietnam War almost 60,000 Americans had died.[5] The United States fought the Vietnam War with modern weapons and

THE TELEVISED WAR

Vietnam was the first war to be fought in the public eye, with images of the war and fighting shown on the nightly television news broadcast. Before Vietnam, wars were reported in the newspapers or in carefully created newsreels that showed in theaters. Such reports were designed to inspire patriotism by showcasing bravery and heroics rather than displaying what it was really like to fight a war. In contrast, television news reports during the Vietnam War showed the wounded and dead and the conditions the war was being fought in. These broadcasts were not censored for the public and made war more shocking. As a result, people were more likely to form negative opinions about the war because they could see what it was actually like.

William Westmoreland, the general who led the US forces in Vietnam between 1964 and 1968, said years later in a *Time* magazine interview: "Vietnam was the first war ever fought without any censorship. Without censorship, things can get terribly confused in the public mind."[6]

Westmoreland's opinion seemed to be that the public would have been better off had it not known so much about the situation in Vietnam. He was implying there would have been less protesting and opposition to the war if the information the public received had been censored as it had been during earlier wars.

tactics, but it was unable to win the war as easily as it might have thought. There did not seem to be any end in sight.

Protesting the War

At the start of the Vietnam War, only a small percentage of Americans were opposed to the country's involvement in Vietnam. But as the war continued and no clear victory seemed to be developing, more and more Americans began to protest US involvement. The first Vietnam War protest march on Washington DC took place in November 1965. Thirty-five thousand people were involved, and it was the first major peace protest up to that point in US history.[7] Two of the students who would find themselves involved in the armband controversy in Des Moines were also at the march, Christopher and John.

Soon others, including university professors and religious groups, began voicing their opposition to Vietnam. Students in colleges and universities also began protesting, and many young men who were eligible to be drafted into the armed forces burned their draft cards in protest.

Beaded necklaces, face paint, and wearing flowers in the hair were some ways members of the counterculture distinguished themselves.

The Vietnam War also turned a more radical and often younger population against an older, more conservative one. The mid-1960s were a time when the hippie counterculture was at its strongest. The hippie movement of the 1960s and 1970s was a subculture of mostly young people who disagreed with the standard rules and values of society and wanted to create a more peaceful, freedom-oriented lifestyle. They created their own counterculture to oppose the culture their parents embraced. Hippies created styles of dress and appearance that made them recognizable to each other as well as set apart from traditional values. The counterculture included things such as growing long hair (both men and women) and wearing bell-bottomed jeans or elements of dress borrowed from other cultures (such as peasant blouses or Native American clothing), sandals or bare feet, no makeup for women, and accessories such as headscarves and beaded necklaces. The counterculture also extended beyond appearance to include a freer attitude toward love and sex and activities such as recreational drug use.

These young hippies vocally opposed the Vietnam War and frequently participated in protests. Young people protested the war all over the United States. Some

Rioters in the Watts neighborhood of Los Angeles crowded a police car on August 12, 1965.

Protests were also taking place in cities across the country. Many cities were suffering from unemployment, poor schools, a lack of public transportation, and uncontrollable crime rates. In the Watts neighborhood of Los Angeles, California, riots erupted for six days in August 1965 as citizens demanded government help.

Many women were also demanding more freedom and opportunities for themselves. Many resented the male-dominated US society of the time, which placed women firmly within the home and felt they should be solely wives and mothers. Women did not have many opportunities to work outside the home or develop careers. This situation led to an increasing number of pickets and demonstrations for women's rights.

Most of the protests taking place in the United States in 1965 involved college students, but they did not generally include high schoolers or younger children. While some high school students adopted some of the marks of protest, such as the long hair, peace symbols, or love beads of the hippie culture, full-fledged antiwar or civil rights demonstrations were unusual. Students who were in high school in 1965 were part of the first generation to grow up with televisions as a constant in their lives. As a result, for the first time, high school students in the 1960s could see the protests of other students across the country on their nightly news. But in a place such as Des Moines, located in the heart of the Midwest, school demonstrations were practically unheard of.

Chapter 3

The Tinker and Eckhardt Families

John, Mary Beth, and Christopher were not rebels within their families. In fact, the three Iowa kids were brought up in homes where free speech and free thinking were valued and encouraged. This familial encouragement set the stage for their decision to protest.

The Eckhardts

Christopher's father, William Eckhardt, was a clinical psychologist and served on the faculty of the College of Osteopathic Medicine and Surgery in Des Moines. His mother, Margaret Eckhardt, was the president of the Des Moines chapter of the Women's International

In 1969, members of the WILPF staged a protest in Denver, Colorado, against the use of nerve gas in the Vietnam War.

League for Peace and Freedom (WILPF). This group was just one part of the family's activities involving a "peace community" of people in Des Moines, including the Tinker family, who worked for world peace and opposed the Vietnam War.

Christopher had an older brother, Edward, and a younger brother, Stephen. They lived a middle-class life

WILPF

The Women's International League for Peace and Freedom (WILPF) was founded in 1915 as the Women's Peace Party. It was part of the suffrage movement in the United States that worked to secure women's rights to vote. The league was also interested in peace and ending the hostilities of World War I. In 1919, it joined the International Women's Congress for Peace and Freedom to form the Women's International League for Peace and Freedom. The WILPF, which still existed in 2012, works for peace, disarmament, and gender equality, as well as a world free from pollution, violence, poverty, and domination.

in a comfortable home in Des Moines. Christopher's mother, Margaret, did not work outside the home but participated in many volunteer activities, while his father supported the family. Christopher was involved in many different school activities and sports.

And yet, because of his family's involvement with the peace movement, Christopher was exposed to meetings and speeches concerning peace and civil rights for most of his childhood. Through his mother's work with the WILPF, he met many famous civil rights advocates when she brought them to Des Moines, such as the African-American politician Julian Bond and the author of the book *Black Like Me*, John Howard Griffin.

THE QUAKERS

The Quaker Church, also known as the Religious Society of Friends or the Friends, is a religious Christian denomination that was formed in England in the seventeenth century. Quakers believe in service and volunteering. The Quaker religion is also known for its opposition to war, which can be seen in one of the statements of their faith that guides them through life: "We utterly deny all outward wars and strife and fighting with outward weapons, for any end or under any pretence [*sic*] whatsoever. And this is our testimony to the whole world."[1] For this reason, Quakers have long been linked with antiwar movements. They also played a key role in the movement to abolish slavery that preceded the Civil War.

Griffin, a white man, had darkened his skin to pose as an African American and wrote *Black Like Me* about the experience. Christopher went with his parents on many civil rights marches in the 1960s. He also helped create a political discussion group at Roosevelt High School, which brought important political figures into the school to talk with students.

The Eckhardt family's involvement in liberal politics also fit with their more liberal religious views. The family had belonged to several different religious groups. Before moving to Des Moines, the family members attended meetings of the Quaker church in North Carolina.

Once in Des Moines, they attended the Unitarian church. The Unitarians sponsored a group called the Liberal Religious Youth (LRY) for teens. LRY was unusual because the young members governed themselves with minimal involvement from adults, who served only as advisers. The LRY organization was known for its involvement in antiwar, counterculture, and civil rights activities throughout the 1960s and 1970s. Christopher was actively involved in the LRY

THE LRY

The Liberal Religious Youth (LRY) organization was founded in 1954 as part of the Unitarian church. This church varies from other Christian churches because of its belief that there is just one God, not the three-part God (Father, Son, and Holy Ghost) that many other Christian churches believe in. The Unitarian church believes Jesus Christ was a prophet, not a part of God. Many Unitarian churches had LRY groups. LRY became known for its involvement with antiwar, counterculture, and civil rights issues. Sometimes the adult church leadership supported the group's activities, but other times the leadership opposed what the group was doing. Eventually, church leadership clashed too often with the liberal LRY groups. The church disbanded the LRY organization in 1982. It was replaced by another youth group, the Young Religious Unitarian Universalists.

group and later served as vice president of another student group, the Unitarian Youth League.

Christopher was also a model student in many ways. He got good grades, served on the student council, participated in sports, and was popular with other students. He was also a Boy Scout and youth leader at his church, and he maintained a snow-shoveling and lawn-mowing business. In fact, on the afternoon when the meeting took place that would launch the armband protest, he only participated in parts of the meeting because he kept leaving to shovel driveways from a recent snow. In most ways, Christopher was a regular kid, not a rebel or an outcast.

The Tinkers

The Tinker family also lived in Des Moines, but in a more working-class neighborhood than the Eckhardts. Their father, Leonard Tinker, was an ordained minister in the Methodist Church. However, he had taken a leave of absence from the Methodist Conference to work as a representative of the American Friends Service Committee (AFSC). The AFSC was affiliated with the Quaker church. The organization worked for peace and social justice in the United States and overseas. Leonard

John and Mary Beth grew up in a family active
in social justice causes.

worked for the AFSC throughout the 1960s and 1970s.
Before moving to Des Moines, the family had lived in
Atlantic, Iowa, where Leonard served as a Methodist

minister. He was asked to leave the town because of the family's political beliefs. Leonard had also been named in an anticommunist brochure that circulated throughout the state at that time, giving him a reputation as a Communist sympathizer. The Tinker family moved to Des Moines, where Leonard worked for the Methodist church before taking his position with the AFSC.

Lorena Jeanne Tinker, John and Mary Beth's mother, was also active in several civil rights groups. She was pursuing a doctorate in psychology at Iowa State University in Ames, Iowa. She once invited an African-American public official to speak to the young adult class she held at the parsonage in Atlantic and then encouraged other members of his family to attend the church. As a result, many members of the church criticized her for her position on racial issues, and the Tinkers were asked to leave their church position.

Both John and Mary Beth and their younger siblings, Hope and Paul, grew up learning the importance their family placed on social activism. Their family had been involved in the antiwar movement their entire lives, ever since their father had received an exemption from serving in World War II because he was a pacifist and a member of the clergy. There was

MEETING MARTIN LUTHER KING JR.

One of the experiences Lorena Tinker told her children about was a conversation she had with Dr. Martin Luther King Jr. after he gave a speech in Des Moines in the mid-1960s. They talked together about the fears they both had of something happening to their children as a result of their work and the controversy that often accompanied it. He asked her if she was ever worried about her children's safety, and she responded that of course she was. But Lorena also told him that she believed that if a cause was important enough, then certain risks, even to children, were unavoidable. As John W. Johnson described the conversation in his book *The Struggle for Student Rights*:

> *King sadly agreed. Then he added that because he and his family were Christians they all believed that if they were killed they'd go to heaven. However, he admitted that that didn't keep his children from hiding under the kitchen table if they were scared.*[3]

also a family tradition of attending antiwar marches and protests. Mary Beth later spoke about traveling with her father during his trips as peace education secretary for the AFSC. "He was giving speeches about peace . . . China and Vietnam mostly. . . . We would go with him and be real proud to be in charge of the literature table."[2] She also remembered her mother telling her about working in the South during the early 1960s and visiting the home of an elderly African-American woman who warned her not to sit next to the window because of the risk of being shot.

Episodes such as these, as well as the marches and protests they attended, helped make the Tinker children as active in the peace movement and the civil rights movement as their parents were. Before John attended North High School, where he was a student when the armband protest took place, he chose to ride a bus across town for his entire ninth grade year simply to attend a school in a part of Des Moines that was more racially mixed. As John later said, "Our family was surrounded by the antiwar movement . . . all of the kids were swept up by it."[4] However, many family friends, even those who were members of the Quaker church and taught their children to be activists, wondered if the Tinkers had started their children in social action at too early an age. Lorena remembered:

> People would say to us, "Why are you taking your children? . . . You're damaging your children or their future." And we said, "We don't think we're damaging them. We're committed to certain values, and we want our children to be part of it, and they would jump in the car and go with us willingly."[5]

John was an average student. He was not involved in sports, but he was a member of his school band and orchestra. Mary Beth was a better student and more popular in school. She was a budding singer who was interested in music, and she was also involved in social activities such as sleepovers at friends' houses.

Backlash

The Tinker children and Christopher were aware of the kinds of negative reactions many civil rights and antiwar protesters often suffered, from verbal abuse to actual physical violence. However, they probably did not believe they were in any danger from simply wearing a black armband, even after being ordered not to do so by school officials. But after local and national papers published news of the armband incident, the families began receiving letters and telephone calls, some supportive but some negative or threatening. The Eckhardts received one note that read, "Go back to

> "I was leaving for school one morning, on my way out the door, and the phone rang and I picked it up. This woman said, IS this Mary Tinker? And I said yes. And she said, I'm going to *kill* you!"[6]
> —MARY BETH TINKER

Russia if you like communism so much."[7] Red paint was thrown at the Tinker house. The family even received a phone call on Christmas Eve during which the caller threatened to bomb their house that night. Another caller told Margaret, "You're looking for trouble and you're going to get it."[8] A radio talk show host even said he would pay for the legal defense of anyone who went after the Tinkers with a shotgun.

As the events of December 16, 1965, moved beyond the walls of the three schools John, Mary Beth, and Christopher attended, a chain of events was set into motion that would ultimately lead to a Supreme Court case. And despite the initial reactions to the incident, the families involved would find that they not only had broader support but that they would eventually become part of US history. ∼

Chapter 4

The School Board Meets

By the evening of December 16, 1965, both Mary Beth and Christopher had been suspended from school. Suspension automatically carried with it grading penalties for any work missed while the student was out and several hours of after-school detention once they were readmitted. But the students and their families knew there were larger issues to consider.

An Earlier Decision

When the principal of Harding Middle School, Chester Pratt, was quoted in the *Des Moines Register* on December 17 about Mary Beth's suspension, he

IN THE NEWS

Des Moines Register, Wednesday Morning,
December 15, 1965

D.M. Schools Ban Wearing Of Viet Truce Armbands

By Jack Magarrell

Des Moines school officials said Tuesday that high school students will not be permitted to wear black armbands at school in support of a truce in Viet Nam. . . .

E. Raymond Peterson, director of secondary education, met with high school principals Tuesday to assure a uniform policy. . . . Peterson said, "For the good of the school system, we don't think this should be permitted. The schools are no place for demonstrations. We allow for free discussion of these things in classes."

Peterson said the decision not to allow students to wear the black armbands was based on a general school policy against "anything that is a disturbing situation within the school."

School officials believe the educational program would be disturbed by the students wearing armbands, he said.[2]

commented, "She was sent home in line with the ban on armbands announced earlier by school officials."[1] School officials had been aware the armband protest was

Robert Kennedy was a strong supporter of civil rights in the United States and abroad.

going to take place. They created the rule in advance specifically to stop the protest.

On December 11, groups of students had held meetings. Some of the people present were members of the LRY group Christopher belonged to, and some were older college students who belonged to the group Students for a Democratic Society (SDS). A classmate of Eckhardt's, Ross Peterson, had written an article for the Roosevelt High School student newspaper announcing their intention to wear the armbands to support Senator Robert Kennedy's proposed Christmas Truce, a 12-hour truce in Vietnam. Ross wrote:

> *Some students who are interested in expressing their grief over the deaths of soldiers and civilians in Vietnam will fast on Thursday, December 16. They will also wear black armbands starting on that same day. . . . [If the United States does not prolong the truce], the armbands will be worn throughout the holiday season.*[3]

When Ross showed his article to the newspaper's adviser, the adviser said there might be problems with it and suggested Ross talk with the principal. Ultimately Ross spoke with the assistant superintendent of schools for Des Moines, who said on December 13 he would not allow the article to be published. Word spread throughout school administrators in the district, and on December 14, the principals of five Des Moines high schools as well as the superintendent of schools and the director of secondary education for the Des Moines school district met to decide on a strategy for handling the protest. At this point they decided to ban armbands from all the schools, not just the high schools.

Because of a brief article in the *Des Moines Register* on Wednesday, December 15, the students were already aware of what the consequences of their actions could be. It seemed to some of them the school administration was creating a double standard: during the previous school year, students had been asked to wear black armbands to signify the loss of school spirit at sports games. Mary Beth herself remembers many times when students attracted no notice at all for wearing buttons for homecoming or national political elections, or even Iron Crosses, which are sometimes a symbol of the Nazi Party and the German army.

A Meeting

On the evening of December 16, Leonard called a meeting at the Eckhardt home to decide how to respond to the suspensions of Mary Beth and Christopher. Approximately 25 people attended the meeting, most of them high school students from Des Moines and their parents. They needed to decide if more students should start wearing armbands and risk being suspended. Most of them felt the students—especially the two who had already been suspended—were being deprived of their opportunity to participate in an expression of free speech.

Iron Crosses are sometimes associated with neo-Nazis and hate groups.

That same night, before the meeting took place, a student from Roosevelt High who was active in the LRY group—it is not known for sure who it was—had called School Board President Niffenegger to request a special meeting of the school board concerning the armband protests. Niffenegger reportedly told the student the issue was not important enough to call a special meeting and it could wait until the next regular school board meeting on December 21. The students knew if they waited until that meeting, and if they were lucky enough to win the right to wear their armbands, then they would only have one day to wear them before school was let out for winter break. It would reduce the effectiveness of the protest.

Knowing the school board would not call a special meeting left the students with only two choices: they could choose not to wear the armbands, since school officials had determined it was an offense punishable by suspension, or they could wear the armbands anyway and risk being sent home. This discussion was particularly relevant for John, who had not worn an armband on the first day hoping the school would reverse its position. Because of his Quaker religious beliefs, John hoped administrators and students could meet, talk, and work out their differences without confrontation. But when Niffenegger called the matter "trivial," John knew there was no hope of a peaceful resolution.[4] He decided to wear the armband to school on the following day.

John wore the armband on Friday, December 17, and he was sent home. He, along with his sister Mary Beth, Christopher, and the other two Roosevelt students, Christine and Bruce, would be the only five students facing consequences because of the armband controversy.

But events had already been set in motion that would bring the issue far beyond the school walls.

The Board Meets

The school board meeting on December 21, 1965, would normally have been a dry, businesslike affair that few non–board members attended. But because of the armband issue and the controversy already brewing around it, this meeting had approximately 200 spectators, including the print and television media, and it was anything but businesslike. Despite what Niffenegger had said, the issue at hand was anything but "unimportant."[5]

SDS members often held protests. One group protested the Vietnam War by standing along the road to President Johnson's Texas home in 1965.

People not directly involved in the school incident were already voicing their opinions. The minister and elders of one Des Moines church had written a letter to Niffenegger, praising him for not allowing the armband protest to take place. Sawyer, the Drake University law professor who would represent the students on behalf of the ICLU, had commented in a *Des Moines Register* article that he expected the board to vote against the protest at their meeting, saying, "I doubt that the school board realizes they have to follow the Constitution."[6]

Students from the Iowa State University SDS chapter even considered picketing the meeting, but in the end they decided it would only alienate parents and they should wait until the board made a formal decision. However, some students did picket the meeting, going against the orders of the SDS group, carrying signs such as "Freedom Means Free Speech" and "Freedom Begins at Home."[7]

Most of the regular business of the meeting was overshadowed by the armband issue. Sawyer challenged the board's right to legally ban armbands in the district, saying it violated the constitutional right to free speech:

> *School board member George Caudill questioned Sawyer's broad support of freedom of expression, asking him if he would also support a student's right to wear a Nazi swastika armband. The combative Sawyer responded quickly, "Yes, and the Jewish Star of David and the Cross of the Catholic church and an arm band saying 'Down with the School Board.'"*[8]

Members of the audience were split widely on the issue. Some military veterans, such as Merle Emerson, a WWII veteran, insisted that schools required discipline and students should not be allowed to do anything

Chapter 5

The School Board Decides

*C*itizens on both sides of the issue were frustrated because the school board had failed to make a decision on the armbands. Sawyer even attempted to get an **injunction** that would lift the ban at least until the board made a decision, but the judge refused because there was only one day left until winter vacation.

In addition to the timing of the school board meetings and vacation, on December 23, 1965, the United States announced it would participate in a brief Christmas Truce. Since the armband protest was supposedly only going to last until a Vietnam truce

THE CHRISTMAS TRUCE

In December 1965, the North Vietnamese offered the United States a truce. Before the United States could formally reply, Senator Robert Kennedy suggested that perhaps the truce could be extended indefinitely and the two sides might have a chance to meet and negotiate, possibly bringing about an end to the Vietnam War. On Christmas, the United States decided to suspend bombing for a 24-hour period and to cease ground fighting until December 26. However, the North Vietnamese did not fully cooperate with the cease-fire, and Americans and South Vietnamese were killed during that time. The United States resumed its bombing in January 1966.

was declared, it would seem that students no longer needed to wear the armbands anyway.

Going National

In the meantime, a story about the Des Moines controversy was published in the *New York Times* on December 23, 1965. "Des Moines Stirs Liberties Protests: Antiwar Armbands Brings Suspensions" just repeated information that had already been published

injunction—A court order ordering someone to do or not do a specified act.

in local Iowa papers. But for a paper as big and as far removed from Iowa as the *New York Times* to run any article on the subject was a hint showing just how big the issue might become.

Closer to home, Niffenegger and Leonard Tinker both appeared on a local television show, *People's Press Conference*, to talk about the armband issue. They both agreed it was appropriate to discuss the Vietnam War

NIFFENEGGER SPEAKS TO THE PRESS

On December 29, 1965, Niffenegger made several statements to the press that particularly angered the Eckhardt and Tinker families. He said,

> It is disturbing to many folks in our community— and it certainly is to me—that the armband demonstration takes place against a background of radical and extremist groups, including American Friends Service Committee, Women's International League for Peace and Freedom, and Students for a Democratic Society.[1]

Niffenegger was basically implying that the involvement of the Tinkers and Eckhardts in some of these organizations was the reason why their children protested in the first place. The two families were also angered that Niffenegger linked the AFSC and the WILPF—two organizations dedicated to peace—with the SDS, which was a much more radical group.

in classrooms, but Niffenegger maintained that protests would only lead to chaos. He said that classroom discussions were better than protests because they were "organized and controlled."[2] Tinker insisted that too much control distracted from the ideals of democracy, saying, "How much control can you have and still have a democratic country?"[3] And when asked why he supported his children in defying a school rule, Tinker replied, "When your children do things that are right, you have to support them."[4]

A Not-So-Public Meeting

While everyone waited for the next regular school board meeting to take place on January 3, 1966, the board was conducting a meeting the public was not invited to. On December 31, 1965, the seven school board members, along with the Des Moines superintendent and the board's attorney, met for lunch at a Des Moines hotel. The sign outside the room read "D.M. School Board Meeting." This was in direct violation of a standing policy that required all board business, other than personnel issues, to be conducted in meetings open to the public. The *Des Moines Register* ran the story two days later, accusing the board of holding a secret meeting for almost four hours.

The board members claimed the meeting needed to be private. It allowed them to ask the board's attorney, Judge Allan Herrick, specific questions about the legality of the suspensions. It was also an opportunity for the board to draft a memorandum arguing that administrators had a legal right to ban armbands. The board did not vote whether to maintain the ban during this "secret" meeting. That would take place at the open meeting in a few days. However, many people, including the League of Women Voters, expressed concern that the board had felt the need to conduct business pertaining to the armband controversy behind closed doors.

Casting Their Votes

After the secret meeting, but before the next public board meeting, the Tinker and Eckhardt families and their children decided the teens would continue to wear their black armbands even though the Christmas Truce had indeed occurred. They felt it was important to wear them to mourn the casualties of the Vietnam War. As a result, John, Mary Beth, and Christopher elected to stay home from school the first day after the vacation. They hoped the school board would vote against the armband restriction and allow them to wear the armbands without fear of punishment.

Mary Beth, John, and Christopher all elected to keep wearing their armbands after the truce was over.

On the evening of January 3, 1966, the second public school board meeting took place. The meeting room was overflowing with spectators. Again the public was allowed to speak for and against the ban, although most of them opposed it. Both the Tinker and Eckhardt families read prepared statements. Christopher commented,

> *The administrators put a ban on the armbands because they believed it would cause a disturbance in the schools. Well, by now you ought to know that the armbands caused no such disturbance in the schools, although the ban itself has caused quite a disturbance in the community.*[5]

CHRISTOPHER'S POEM

Christopher later wrote a poem about the armband controversy for a school assignment. It was a parody of "Mary Had a Little Lamb." The poem earned an A. It began:

Harold has a black arm band,

As black as black could be.

Everywhere that Harold went,

That band was there to see.[6]

But when all the arguments both supporting and denouncing the armband policy were done, the board's vote was 5–2 in favor of upholding the school administrators' ban on wearing armbands in Des Moines schools.

The ICLU Steps In

Sawyer, the first ICLU attorney who acted as spokesman for the families in the armband case, was joined by another ICLU attorney, Val Schoenthal. Together they visited the Eckhardt home after the school board's decision. Many of the supporters of the armband protest were there. The adults congratulated the three teenagers for their actions so far and for how they had challenged the thinking of many people in the area about civil liberties. That in itself was an important achievement. Surprisingly, the attorneys also urged John, Mary Beth, and Christopher to return to school without the armbands so the school administrations and the school board would not be provoked any more. However, the three were upset and, at the suggestion of ICLU attorneys, they agreed to wear black clothing for days (or in John's case, months) following the decision. When asked for his reaction to this, Niffenegger reportedly said, "Well, I guess we'll have to let them keep their clothes on."[7]

During these early weeks of 1966, the ICLU and the families of the students had to decide whether to take their case to court. It seemed fairly obvious to everyone that taking the case to court was never really in doubt, but the ICLU wanted to be sure the families would be prepared for the legal battle. The ICLU agreed to provide some financial support to help the families with court fees, as well as cover the cost of hiring Dan Johnston as their attorney. Soon Johnston began putting together the **lawsuit** they would bring against the school district. It was filed on March 14, 1966, on behalf of Christopher, John, Mary Beth, and their fathers as next friends. The suit named as **defendants** the seven school board members, the superintendent, the principals of the schools, and a few other teachers and administrators, for a total of 23. The legal fight had begun. ~

defendant—The person against whom legal action is brought.

lawsuit—Legal action brought against a party.

Chapter 6

District Court Trial

ohnston prepared an eight-page complaint
for the suit against the Des Moines school
board. It stated the basis for the claim (the events
of December 16 and 17) and the section of US
law that applied to the situation, in this case a
law concerning the deprivation of citizens' rights
secured by the US Constitution. The suit noted
that the three **plaintiffs** were all US citizens,
they were minors, and they were enrolled in the
Des Moines school system. This established that
they were covered by the section of law Johnston
was using to bring the suit against the school district.
The law required that the defendants be citizens of

PROTECTING PEOPLE'S RIGHTS

The section of US law that was relevant to the *Tinker* case is Title 42, US Code, Section 1983. Today, it reads:

Every person who, under color of any statute, ordinance, regulation, custom, or usage, of any State . . . subjects, or causes to be subjected, any citizen of the United States or other person within the jurisdiction thereof to the deprivation of any rights, privileges, or immunities secured by the Constitution and laws, shall be liable to the party injured in an action at law, suit in equity, or other proper proceeding for redress.[1]

Passed in 1871, this law was originally intended to protect citizens from state agencies, or people acting under the jurisdiction of state agencies, from violence or having their rights taken away. It means the constitutional rights of citizens are protected and these agencies (in this case, the Des Moines school district) can be liable in a lawsuit for depriving someone of his or her First Amendment rights.

the United States and residing in the territory belonging to the US **District Court** of the Southern District of Iowa, as well as going to school under the

district court—A court that hears cases for federal crimes.
plaintiff—The person who charges another with wrongdoing.

71

Wearing armbands was a frequent form of student protest; Harvard University students wore armbands to protest in 1969.

jurisdiction of the school district being sued. Johnston's complaint made it clear the case met these requirements.

Johnston ended the complaint by saying the three plaintiffs were "lawfully and peacefully engaged in the exercise of the right of free speech secured for them by the Amendments One and Fourteen of the United States Constitution."[2] Johnston requested that the court issue a permanent injunction against the school district, allowing students to wear armbands without fear of punishment and to be reinstated in school. It also asked for a small amount of money: court costs plus nominal damages of one dollar.

Following the filing of the suit, the people named as defendants in the case were served with copies of the complaint. This meant they were formally notified of the lawsuit against them, and notified about what they would need to do as a result of the complaint. On April 29, 1966, the attorney for the school board, Herrick, filed a three-page answer to the suit on behalf of the defendants. It ended with a short statement expressing the defendants' legal argument:

jurisdiction—The authority to govern or try cases; also refers to the territory under that authority.

The wearing of said armbands was done in direct violation of the reasonable rules for the regulation of conduct of students . . . and to permit continued violation of said rules and regulations threatened a breakdown in the discipline and orderly conduct of classes in said respective schools.[3]

It then requested the complaint be dismissed.

Going to Trial

The case would be tried in a federal court because any case involving government organizations accused of disobeying the US Constitution or its amendments automatically begins as a federal trial without a **jury**. The case became known as *Tinker v. Des Moines Independent Community School District*. The school year was ending in Des Moines. Meanwhile, Judge Roy L. Stephenson of the US District Court of the Southern District of

US DISTRICT COURTS

US district courts are the first level of federal courts to hear criminal and civil cases. Most federal court cases begin at this level. There are 94 district courts, with at least one in every state. Some larger states have as many as four district courts. Judges are appointed by the president and approved by the Senate as specified in the Constitution.

Iowa asked the attorneys for a pretrial conference. This was a procedure often used in federal cases that allowed the judge to work with the attorneys before the trial so that the proceedings would take place as smoothly and efficiently as possible. Sometimes it was possible for parties to settle their disputes during these conferences, but not in the *Tinker v. Des Moines* case. Stephenson then ordered the two attorneys to prepare a trial **brief**, provide lists of witnesses for the trial, and take **depositions**.

The two briefs were submitted in July. Their purpose was to provide the judge with the facts of the case and the legal issues that pertained to it, and they would give the judge something to study along with the **testimony** from the plaintiffs and defendants. The briefs, along with the depositions taken during the summer, were the last preparations that needed to be made before the trial could begin.

brief—A document that establishes the legal argument of a case.

deposition—A recorded out-of-court interview that takes place under oath.

jury—A group of people selected to deliver a verdict on an issue, such as a court case.

testimony—Something declared in court under oath.

JUDGE STEPHENSON

Judge Roy Stephenson was 49 years old at the time of the *Tinker v. Des Moines* trial. He had been appointed to the US District Court of the Southern District of Iowa, in 1960 by President Dwight D. Eisenhower. Before he became a judge, Stephenson was an attorney in Des Moines. He was an active member of the Republican Party and had also been a high-ranked officer in the army, serving in World War II. He had received several medals during that time. Lawyer Johnston felt Stephenson's military background and conservative politics may have influenced his ruling in the *Tinker* case, since the judge likely would not be favorably disposed to war protesters or students who went against school authority. Johnston also tried later cases about draft evasion before Judge Stephenson and noted that the judge found it very difficult to sympathize with any form of antiwar protest.

It was Monday, July 25, 1966. The news about the Vietnam War had been especially bad preceding the trial, with headlines telling of US planes and pilots shot down and 737 American deaths in just one week.[4] Despite President Lyndon Johnson's assurance that the North Vietnamese were being gradually worn down by the US forces, no one felt particularly good about what was going on. In the Des Moines Federal Court Building, Judge Stephenson called the court to order to officially begin the trial. It would be a trial without a jury, since

The *Tinker* case first came to trial at a time when the conflict in Vietnam was going badly for the United States.

it was not a criminal case. Nonjury trials are especially efficient in situations in which the case involves legal issues more than the facts of an event because an experienced judge will issue a judgment on the case and the lawyers do not have to explain the case to a jury.

The courtroom held the plaintiffs and defendants, their lawyers, the Tinker and Eckhardt families, and members of the Des Moines "peace community," those people who had served in various organizations with the two families and supported them.

Judge Stephenson opened the proceedings by acknowledging he had read the two lawyers' briefs. He asked the lawyers if they wanted to present opening statements about the case. They declined, and then Johnston called his first witness, John.

John was asked basic questions about himself and school. He recounted all the details of the day he wore the armband to school. When Johnston asked him if he and his family ever talked about the Vietnam War at home, he replied, "Quite often. I talk about war and peace with my parents and most of my brothers and sisters, although I don't agree with all of my parents' views."[5]

John's answer helped Johnston establish that he had been acting on his own and had not been pushed into wearing an armband by his parents. It was important to make it clear these students had been acting on their own free will—and not just according to their parents' wishes—to make the case that students in schools had the right to free speech. When a lawyer for the school district, Philip Lovrien, **cross-examined** John, he tried to show John's decision was actually his parents' idea by stressing that John's parents were present at most of the meetings during which the armband decision was made. He also used John's testimony to show that John had openly broken a school rule by wearing the armband and also tried to show that wearing it had attracted attention and possibly created an explosive situation.

> " When people are getting killed it's important to me."[6]
>
> —*JOHN TINKER ON WHY HE WORE A BLACK ARMBAND TO SCHOOL*

cross-examined—Questioned the witness second in order to check or discredit the witness's original testimony.

Mary Beth was called as the next witness and explained the events of the day she wore the armband. She was questioned about where the cloth for the armbands came from—around her house. She affirmed that her mother had purchased it, a fact the school district lawyers used to link the armband situation to the parents, not the students.

Both sides then questioned Christopher. His testimony was important to the school district defendants because his experiences showed there were disruptive incidents in school that occurred as a result of his wearing an armband. His testimony was the longest and caused the most debate.

The Defendants Speak

Johnston questioned six of the defendants from the Des Moines school district, starting with Donald Wetter, the principal of North High School. During Herrick's cross-examination, Wetter told his version of his meeting with John and emphasized that he had told John he would do everything in his power to protect John's rights and his welfare. He suggested to John it might be a better expression of his feelings toward the war if

FOURTEENTH AMENDMENT ARGUMENTS

Part of Johnston's argument about the rights of the students to free speech included the Fourteenth Amendment as well as the First Amendment.

The Fourteenth Amendment, Section 1:

All persons born or naturalized in the United States, and subject to the jurisdiction thereof, are citizens of the United States and of the State wherein they reside. No State shall make or enforce any law which shall abridge the privileges or immunities of citizens of the United States; nor shall any State deprive any person of life, liberty, or property, without due process of law; nor deny to any person within its jurisdiction the equal protection of the laws.[7]

This meant that the students had the right to free speech under the federal provisions of the First Amendment, and they had the same right within their state and under state law. The state of Iowa could not use a state law to deny them free speech on a state level. Together the First and Fourteenth Amendments protect citizens' right to free speech at both the state and federal level.

he participated in a Veteran's Day or Memorial Day ceremony instead of wearing an armband.

Vice Principal Donald Blackman of Roosevelt High School was questioned about his interactions with Christopher. Johnston asked him whether he had ever seen any other students wearing potentially distracting or controversial symbols, such as political buttons, antiwar pins, or Iron Crosses. Blackman admitted he might have seen these items worn by students, but said he really had not paid attention. Johnston asked, "Was the armband rule the first rule against wearing political or religious symbols in the Des Moines Schools?" to which Blackman responded, "Yes." [8] This established the plaintiff's position that the administrators' ruling on the black armbands was unfair because other political and religious symbols had never been censored. The lawyers questioned several other witnesses. Finally, Niffenegger testified about the school board meetings and their chaotic atmosphere that made him think students wearing armbands was a potentially explosive situation in a school.

A Decision

The court adjourned on July 26, 1966, after the lawyers' closing arguments. Judge Stephenson did not issue his decision in the case until September 1, 1966. In his written memorandum opinion, he said:

> *The question which now must be determined is whether the action of officials of the defendant*

*school district forbidding the wearing of arm bands on school facilities deprived the plaintiffs of constitutional rights secured by the freedom of speech clause of the first amendment. An individual's right of free speech is protected against state infringement by the **due process** clause of the fourteenth amendment. The wearing of an arm band for the purpose of expressing certain views is a symbolic act and falls within the protection of the first amendment's free speech clause.*[9]

In other words, the court agreed that when the students wore the armbands, they were protected by the free speech part of the First Amendment. The opinion continued:

However, the protections of that clause are not absolute. . . . Officials of the defendant school district have the responsibility for maintaining a scholarly, disciplined atmosphere within the classroom. These officials not only have a right, they have an obligation to prevent anything which might be disruptive of such an atmosphere. Unless

---

due process—A basic principle in the US legal system that requires fairness in the government's dealings with people.

TESTIFYING

In 1998, Christopher talked about what it was like for him to testify in court:

> What was it like for a 13 year old, 15 year old, and 16 year old to go to trial to contest your suspension? First, to set one part of the record straight, Mary Beth was 13, John was 15, and although 99% of the literature for the past 30+ years wants to age me to being 16, I, like John, was only 15 years old. But, who's counting? At one point when I was on the witness stand, I testified how the Vice-Principal of Roosevelt, on 12–16–65, asked me to remove my black arm band, and I refused on constitutional grounds. Then he asked me, "Do you want a busted nose?" While repeating this, I watched from the witness stand, as the Vice-Principal walked out of the courtroom. I still don't know whether it was out of shame, or just maybe because he needed to go to the bathroom.[11]

the actions of school officials in this connection are unreasonable, the Courts should not interfere.[10]

Here the court said, however, that even though the students' actions are protected as free speech, the fact that they are students in a school gives the school officials the right to restrict free speech if they feel it might cause a dangerous or disruptive situation. As the opinion explained:

School officials must be given a wide discretion and if, under the circumstances, a disturbance in school discipline is reasonably to be anticipated, actions which are reasonably calculated to prevent such a disruption must be upheld by the Court. In the case now before the Court, the regulation of the defendant school district was, under the circumstances, reasonable and did not deprive the plaintiffs of their constitutional right to freedom of speech.[12]

The judge clearly felt that the school officials were acting properly in restricting a situation they thought might be disruptive and that these reasonable actions did not deprive the students of their rights. He denied the plaintiffs' request for an injunction and damages and told them they would be paying the court costs. Judge Stephenson had ruled against the Tinkers and Eckhardt and in favor of the school district. The district court case was closed. ∽

Chapter 7

Court of Appeals Proceedings

ohnston was not particularly surprised they lost their case in district court. He had already suspected Judge Stephenson's background might make him unsympathetic to the armband incidents. But he did feel pleased it was now on record in the court proceedings that the school district had essentially punished the students for wearing armbands but had never used the same punishment or any punishment at all for students who had worn religious or political symbols in the past. It was a double standard he felt a higher court might find a problem with. On the other hand, the defendants' attorney felt they had succeeded in showing that wearing armbands had seriously

Should a school be allowed to ban some types of personal expression while allowing others?

threatened discipline in the Des Moines schools and that the judge's written decision underlined how important that aspect of the case was.

An Appeal

Neither family was ready to accept the decision and give up on the case. The next step in the process was to take the case to the next level: the Eighth Circuit US Court of Appeals. This was the part of the judicial system that occupied a tier between the district court and the US Supreme Court. A court of appeals does not conduct a trial based on the facts of the case. Instead, it holds hearings on the legal points that were raised in lower courts. For an **appeal** to proceed, there must be a possibility that the lower court committed an error.

appeal—A petition submitted to a higher court to review the decision or proceedings of a lower court.

COURT OF APPEALS

The US circuit court of appeals is the next step up from US district court. Any party who is dissatisfied with the judgment of a district court can appeal to the court of appeals in their geographical district. There are 13 US circuit courts of appeal, 12 of them located in districts around the country. The last is located in Washington DC. Because the facts of a case have already been determined by the lower district court, the court of appeals will only examine the record of the lower court for errors in the law. It does not review the basic facts of the case or gather any additional testimony. Usually, a panel of three judges will rule on a given case. The court of appeals decision usually will be the last word in a case, unless it sends the case back to the trial court for additional proceedings or the parties ask the US Supreme Court to review the case.

The ICLU agreed to continue funding the legal process by assisting the families with court costs. So with the agreement of the families involved, Johnston filed a notice of appeal. Again, Johnston and the attorneys for the Des Moines school district wrote briefs for the judges, explaining the case and why they felt the lower court's decision was in error or why it was correct. These legalities were a long, slow process. Finally the case was assigned to a panel of three judges. The hearing in the court of appeals was set for April 1967.

The attorneys in the case, Johnston for the Tinker and Eckhardt families and Herrick and Lovrien for the school district, presented their **oral arguments** in front of the panel of judges. The Tinker and Eckhardt families and the Des Moines school district people were not required to attend the hearing because the appeals court would gather no new evidence. Instead, the court used the facts and testimony gathered in the lower court case. And yet, after hearing the arguments and reading the briefs, the three judges could not make a decision on *Tinker v. Des Moines*. So a reargument of the case was ordered to take place in October 1967, before the Eighth Circuit judges **en banc**. An en banc hearing was rare, and the court noted that it was ordering the hearing because of the importance of the case. At the October hearing, the attorneys once again gave their oral arguments, but this time they spoke in front of eight judges instead of three.

The *Des Moines Register* published an article about the en banc hearing, which is the only record of the case because there was no official transcript created. At one point, one of the judges challenged Johnston by saying that school officials would be likely to consider "alternate points of view . . . expressed in class, where it's regulated." Johnston responded by saying, "I submit this is not free speech at all. There is too much interference. What if President Johnson said you can argue against his policies only on Fridays?"[2]

The court's decision came down in November 3, 1967. The en banc court of eight judges had split on the issue, 4–4. When a court of appeals was equally divided on a case, it meant the original decision of the lower court (Judge Stephenson's decision) was automatically upheld. The ruling that upheld the school district's ban on armbands was still in effect. The en banc court issued a **per curiam opinion**. Sometimes a per curiam opinion

en banc—Before the full court, generally all the judges appointed to a given district or circuit.

oral argument—A spoken presentation of a legal case by a lawyer.

per curiam opinion—An opinion issued by the entire court as a whole, not attributed to any single judge.

is issued when the group of judges wishes to withhold the reasons why the court disagreed. The opinion did not analyze the case, nor did it say why the court was split.

Johnston and the families of the students were disappointed by the ruling. However, Johnston realized the opinion of the Eighth Circuit court, which had upheld the lower court decision, meant that the Eighth Circuit court's ruling was in conflict with two Fifth Circuit US Court of Appeals rulings. These other rulings involved the wearing of "freedom buttons." The freedom button rulings made by the Fifth Circuit court also had to do with students and freedom of speech in schools. Both cases were about students wearing freedom buttons inscribed with the acronym SNCC, which meant "Student Non-Violent Coordinating Committee."

In *Burnside v. Byars*, the court of appeals ruled that the school district that prohibited students from wearing the buttons had violated their freedom of expression. But in another similar case, the same court reached an opposite conclusion. It was these two conflicting rulings by one circuit court, in conjunction with the ruling in the Eighth Circuit court, that made Johnston feel the *Tinker* case had a chance of being heard in the Supreme Court.

Writ of Certiorari

Johnston would need to file a petition for a **writ of certiorari** to ask the Supreme Court to review the case. It was not certain whether it would be granted. The Supreme Court typically hears only cases involving an important legal principle or when two or more lower courts have interpreted a law differently. According to Rule 10 of *Rules of the US Supreme Court*, "Review on writ of certiorari is not a matter of right, but a judicial discretion. A petition for writ of certiorari will be granted only for compelling reasons."[3] Would the *Tinker* case be compelling enough?

The circumstances seemed to fit the *Tinker* case perfectly, since appeals courts had reached different rulings on similar cases. On November 17, 1967, the Eighth Circuit US Court of Appeals gave Johnston an order that put their earlier decision on hold for 30 days.

---

writ of certiorari—An order from a higher court to a lower court calling for the record of a case for review.

WRIT OF CERTIORARI

In 1967, Johnston's petition for a writ of certiorari was one of 1,532 filed during the year. The Supreme Court granted writs to only 156 cases.[4] Today, more than 7,000 petitions are filed each year, but even fewer are granted than were in 1967. It takes a vote of four of the nine justices to grant certiorari. Most justices rely on their clerks to determine which petitions seem worthy of the Supreme Court.

This time would allow him time to petition the Supreme Court for the writ of certiorari.

On March 4, 1968, everyone involved in the case finally got an answer. The clerk of the Supreme Court issued an "order allowing certiorari" in the case of *Tinker v. Des Moines Independent Community School District.* Five Supreme Court **justices** had voted in favor of hearing the case and four against. The Supreme Court would hear the case. ～

justice—A member of the US Supreme Court.

Mary Beth's mother continued to support her daughter through the trials and appeals process.

Chapter 8

The Supreme Court Hears the Case

It had been almost three years since the armband incident took place in the Des Moines schools. The legal system moved slowly, and it was not until November 12, 1968, that the Supreme Court of the United States heard arguments in the case of *Tinker v. Des Moines*.

The Country in 1968

In January 1968, the North Vietnamese launched an attack during the Vietnamese holiday Tet, killing many US soldiers. This military action is known as the Tet Offensive. The Tet Offensive is often considered a turning point in Americans' attitudes toward the war. More Americans began to realize the country was not winning the war in Vietnam.

In April 1968, civil rights leader Martin Luther King Jr. was assassinated in Memphis, Tennessee. In June, Senator Robert Kennedy was assassinated after giving a speech in California.

By the fall of 1968, the situation in Vietnam had grown even worse. More than 500,000 Americans were serving in Vietnam.[1] Thirty thousand had died fighting there.[2] Antiwar protests on college campuses were getting larger and more frequent, and more involved violence. In October, President Johnson ordered the bombing of North Vietnam be halted, hoping he could step up peace talks with the North Vietnamese. However, his efforts failed because the South Vietnamese refused to negotiate with the North Vietnamese Communist National Liberation Front. President Johnson did not seek reelection, and the new president-elect that November was Richard Nixon.

It had been a year of dramatic changes as well as an increasing number of protests. Women's liberation was a growing movement, and there were many related

King's assassination was one of many upheavals
that occurred in 1968.

protests and demonstrations. Free speech was in the spotlight. And as the year drew to a close, the question of whether students had a right to freedom of speech in their schools would finally be decided.

November 12

Christopher and his parents, as well as most of the members of the Tinker family, were present in the courtroom of the Supreme Court building in Washington DC to witness the oral arguments in their case. John was not able to make it from the Midwest in time due to bad weather and missed flights. Once

TINKER BRIEFS

Three briefs were submitted to the Supreme Court before the hearing of *Tinker v. Des Moines*. As before, the first two were written by the Tinker side and the school district side. A third brief was an amicus curiae, which means "friend of the court." It is usually submitted by a third party that is not actually involved in the case but has an interest in the outcome. For the *Tinker* case, an amicus curiae brief was submitted by the United States National Student Association (NSA), a group of college and university student governments. Because so many antiwar protests were taking place on college campuses, the NSA was very interested in the Supreme Court's ruling on student freedom of expression.

again, Johnston and Herrick represented their clients and would argue their cases.

In the months preceding the hearing, both sides submitted briefs outlining their position. During oral arguments in Supreme Court cases, each side is usually allowed only 30 minutes to argue its position. The lawyers prepared extensively for their oral arguments and practiced them in front of other lawyers for their criticism and suggestions. Both lawyers also had to be prepared to answer questions from the Supreme Court justices and to act with respect and deference. Some of the justices had a reputation for being helpful and reassuring with lawyers who were nervous. **Chief Justice** Earl Warren in particular had a reputation for being sympathetic. Johnston remembered thinking humorously, "If anything went really bad, [Chief Justice] Earl Warren would come down off the bench and put his arm around [me]."[3]

Presiding over the court that day was Chief Justice Warren. The other eight associate justices were Hugo Black, William J. Brennan Jr., William O. Douglas, Abe

chief justice—The presiding judge of the US Supreme Court.
   presiding—Hearing and overseeing a legal proceeding.

Fortas, John M. Harlan II, Thurgood Marshall, Potter
Stewart, and Byron White.

Opening Statements

Johnston started the proceedings with his oral argument,
summing up the circumstances of the armband protest
and the legal proceedings that had happened since. After
only five minutes, he was interrupted by Justice White,
who asked him questions about whether the students
had wanted to convey a message by wearing their
armbands. It is typical for justices to ask questions during
Supreme Court hearings, but White asked questions
faster than Johnston could reply. Court transcripts show
White asked 19 separate questions in just three minutes.
As more justices began asking questions, Johnston had
to give up on his prepared presentation and slip his
points into the answers he was giving the justices instead.
This is not uncommon; lawyers often must give their
arguments by responding to questions rather than giving
their prepared remarks. However, Johnston also had to
deal with a series of hostile questions from Justice Black.
Black had misread the records of the original trial and
assumed Mary Beth's wearing of an armband had created
a disruption in her algebra class, which was not true.
Johnston attempted to correct him and made the point

HUGO BLACK

By the time of the *Tinker v. Des Moines* case, Justice Hugo Black was in his eighties and had a reputation for being crotchety and impatient with younger people. Along with Justice William O. Douglas, Black was a strong supporter of First Amendment rights, but he was more hesitant about granting these rights to minors. He disagreed with allowing students to use school as a platform for their political opinions. Black noted, "I have never believed that any person has a right to give speeches or engage in demonstrations where he pleases and when he pleases."[4] He thought the younger generation was running wild and believed there was too much permissiveness in the country.

that if the students' activities had disrupted the school it would have been an entirely different issue.

Herrick's oral arguments covered three constitutional issues: whether teachers have to wait for a disruption to occur or if they can use their judgment to prevent trouble before it starts; how far the judicial system should go in questioning the discretion of school officials; and whether school disturbances should be measured by the same standard as protests on the streets or in other public places. He finished by pointing out that US courts have often claimed that freedom of expression is not a given and has to be balanced against the need to keep order.

He was then questioned by Justice Marshall:

Q (Marshall): How many [students] were wearing armbands?

A (Herrick): There were five suspended for wearing armbands.

Q: Any wearing armbands that were not suspended?

A: Yes, sir, I think there were two.

Q: That makes seven . . . seven out of 18,000? And the School Board was advised that seven students wearing armbands were disrupting 18,000? Am I correct?[5]

Christopher remembered that after this exchange, Justice Marshall just sat back in his chair and shook his head over that particular argument from the school district. "When I heard Justice Thurgood Marshall ask the

> " I think, your honor, that the correct answer to that [question] is free discussion in the classroom is always permitted, always has been, if they want to come in and discuss these matters. But the question of imposing on a captive audience moving in with an armband when it's known through the press, through the community, through the things that have happened here that the community is inflamed might disrupt the orderly conduct of schools."[6]
>
> —*EXCHANGE BETWEEN HERRICK AND CHIEF JUSTICE WARREN, NOVEMBER 12, 1968*

question—'seven out of 18,000, and the school board was afraid that seven students wearing armbands would disrupt 18,000. Am I correct?'—then I was confident we would prevail," Christopher later recalled.[7] Lorena Tinker remembered thinking most of the justices seemed to be sympathetic to Johnston and hostile toward Herrick, especially once Herrick expressed anger over students daring to defy the school authorities. One justice also grilled Herrick about whether the school board had any evidence of a disruption as a result of the arm bands:

> Q: (unnamed Justice): Would I be correct in assuming that if violence had occurred at any of the three schools, the Des Moines school officials would have known about it?
>
> A: (Herrick) I wouldn't want to say this is true because I wouldn't know.
>
> Q: Would it be normal? And my second question would be if the school board knew about it, wouldn't they put in evidence about it? What evidence did the School Board…[cite]…when they adopted this **resolution**? Is it on paper any place?
>
> A: No . . .[8]

Lorena also noted that Justice Marshall seemed to be falling asleep during several points in the lawyers' presentations. As the oral arguments and rebuttals were completed, the case was officially submitted to the court for their consideration. The presentations and questioning were over, and then the waiting began again.

Behind the Scenes

Several days after the arguments were over, the justices gathered to discuss the case. Discussion, according to tradition, took place in a private conference room. It began with the chief justice and went in order by seniority, ending with the most recent member of the court. When voting finally took place, however, it was done from most junior to most senior member and ended with the chief justice. This way, the junior justices would not be swayed by the votes of the more senior justices. Chief Justice Warren's court was also known to be informal, and discussion of cases often took place freely. Once voting took place, the chief justice would assign a justice who voted with the majority to write

resolution—A formal intention or opinion voted on by a lawmaking group or other body.

SUPREME COURT CONFERENCE ROOM

The conference room of the Supreme Court justices is a beautiful room with wood paneling, a chandelier, a fireplace, and a complete bound set of the volumes that contain all of the court's decisions. The justices meet there about two times a week to discuss certiorari petitions, talk about current and upcoming cases, and go through other kinds of business. They sit in chairs around a table, with the chief justice at one end, the chief associate justice (the next most important justice) on the other end, and the rest in between. No one else is allowed inside, not even clerks, aides, or visitors, and the lowest-ranking justice guards the door and receives any messages.

the **majority opinion** for the court. Out of those in the minority, a justice would also be chosen to write a **dissent**, explaining why they did not agree with the majority opinion.

The justices in the *Tinker* case spoke for both sides. Some favored reversing the lower court's ruling and allowing the armbands to be worn, while others wanted to uphold the lower court ruling. According to Peter Irons in his book *The Courage of Their Convictions*:

> *Chief Justice Warren argued . . . that school officials had picked out only one message to censor and thus violated the "equal protection" clause of*

the Fourteenth Amendment. If schools "allowed wearing of Fascist crosses" and political campaign buttons, they could not outlaw Mary Tinker's arm band. Justice Byron White urged that the decision rest on the First Amendment, agreeing with Dan Johnston that "there's no evidence" of disruption in the classrooms.[9]

However, Justice Black's opinion was that the decision of the lower courts should be upheld. Justice Marshall's notes from the conference captured some of Black's remarks, such as "children being allowed to run riot." Justice Douglas's notes also quoted Black: ". . . schools are in great trouble . . . children need discipline . . . the country's going to ruin."[10] It was clear how Black would be voting.

Once voting took place on the case, it would be several more months before the Supreme Court publicly announced its ruling. The justices needed this time to write and approve drafts of the majority and dissenting

dissent—An official written statement of a Supreme Court justice who disagrees with the majority decision.

majority opinion—An explanation of the reasoning behind the majority decision of the Supreme Court.

opinions. As 1968 became 1969, those involved in the case were still wondering just what the vote—and the opinions—would be. ～

Supreme Court justices meet in this conference room to discuss cases in private.

Chapter 9

The Decision

*I*n the early months of 1969, events around the nation and in Vietnam continued to escalate. Major riots and demonstrations took place on many college campuses. President Nixon agreed there needed to be a new "get tough" policy when it came to student demonstrators, but at the same time, he was seen as not living up to his campaign promise of ending the Vietnam War. More than 500,000 US troops were in Vietnam at this time, and the Pentagon planned to continue drafting more young men.[1]

In the midst of this continued unrest and a war that did not seem to be going away, the Supreme Court finally made its decision on *Tinker v. Des Moines*. February 24, 1969, seemed like just another business day in the court, with certiorari granted and denied, orders issued in seven pending cases, and opinions handed down for 20 other cases. But among all this business, the *Tinker* case was getting the most attention.

The Court's Opinion

The official opinion, written by Justice Fortas, was just a little more than 11 pages in the official record, relatively short for a case involving the US Constitution. The first part of the opinion introduced the students and the case. On the third page, Fortas first hints that perhaps the students would succeed when he notes that the district court was correct when it "recognized that the wearing of an armband for the purpose of expressing certain views is the type of symbolic act that is within the Free Speech Clause of the First Amendment."[2] Fortas then went on to make one of the most lasting statements of the Supreme Court's opinion:

> *First Amendment rights, applied in light of the special characteristics of the school environment, are available to teachers and students. It can hardly be argued that either students or teachers shed their constitutional rights to freedom of speech or expression at the schoolhouse gate.*[3]

Justice Fortas served on the Supreme Court from 1965 to 1969.

Fortas went on to say the school officials both banned the armbands and attempted to punish the students who wore them even though their expression of their opinions was silent and did not disrupt classes or the school day. The court case, therefore, did not concern "speech or action that intrudes upon the work of the schools or the rights of other students."[4] The opinion then said:

> The District Court concluded that the action of the school authorities was reasonable because it was based upon their fear of a disturbance from the wearing of the armbands. But, in our system, undifferentiated fear or apprehension of disturbance is not enough to overcome the right to freedom of expression. . . . Any word spoken, in class, in the lunchroom, or on the campus, that deviates from the views of another person may start an argument or cause a disturbance. But our Constitution says we must take this risk; and our history says that it is this sort of hazardous freedom—this kind of openness—that is the basis of our national strength.[5]

Fortas finished by saying, "In the circumstances, our Constitution does not permit officials of the State

In writing his opinion for the Supreme Court' decision, Justice Fortas avoided using the word *war* in his description of the armband protests. Justice Stewart was concerned about using the word *war* to describe the events in Vietnam, since the US Congress had never officially declared war on North Vietnam. He asked Fortas not to use the word in the opinion. Instead, Fortas referred to the United States' part in the Vietnam situation as "hostilities," "conflict," and "involvement."[7]

to deny their form of expression."[6] The decision had been made: the vote was 7–2 in favor of the Tinkers and Eckhardt, with only Justices Black and Harlan voting against. As the opinion has since been interpreted, students have First Amendment protections at school, provided their expressions do not cause a disruption. Three and a half years after the students made their quiet protest, they had finally been vindicated.

Dissenting Opinions

The two justices who voted against the *Tinker* case also wrote their dissenting opinions for the record. Justice Harlan wrote a concise dissenting statement, saying that while he agreed school districts should not be exempt from the Fourteenth Amendment and the requirements for freedom of expression, he also believed schools should be allowed the authority to maintain order:

> *To translate that proposition into a workable constitutional rule, I would, in cases like this, cast upon those complaining the burden of showing that a particular school measure was motivated by other than legitimate school concerns—for example, a desire to prohibit the expression of an unpopular point of view, while permitting expression of the dominant opinion.*[8]

In other words, it should be the responsibility of the students making the complaint to prove the school was acting out of a desire to suppress an opinion rather than to keep order. And because Justice Harlan did not see anything in the previous court cases that showed the Des Moines school district was not acting in good faith, but simply trying to maintain order, he voted to uphold the rulings of the lower courts.

Justice Black, however, was much more critical of the students involved in the *Tinker v. Des Moines* case. His written dissent began with:

> *The Court's holding in this case ushers in what I deem to be an entirely new era in which the power to control pupils by the elected "officials of state*

Justice Harlan served on the Supreme Court for 16 years.

supported public schools . . ." in the United States is in ultimate effect transferred to the Supreme Court.[9]

Black then went on to say:

In my view, teachers in state-controlled public schools are hired to teach there. . . . Certainly a teacher is not paid to go into school and teach subjects the State does not hire him to teach as a part of its selected curriculum. Nor are public school students sent to the schools at public expense to broadcast political or any other views to educate and inform the public. . . . It may be that the Nation has outworn the old-fashioned slogan that "children are to be seen not heard," but one may, I hope, be permitted to harbor the thought that taxpayers send children to school on the premise that at their age they need to learn, not teach.[10]

In other words, Black felt students were in school to learn, not to express their opinions, and their teachers were not hired to teach about subjects not in the curriculum, such as antiwar protests. He also believed students should learn without questioning or

Chief Justice Warren, *right*, congratulated Black on his eightieth birthday in 1966. Black served on the court from 1937 to 1971.

discussion, not raising their voices but only listening to their teachers.

Both sides had spoken, but the majority of the court had clearly agreed with Eckhardt and the Tinkers. An order was then filed with the Eighth US Circuit Court of Appeals, directing that the Tinker petitioners should receive $326.65—$150 for court costs and $176.65 for "printing the record," which was the cost of printing and binding the written transcript of the case—to recover their cost. With that final ruling, *Tinker v. Des Moines* was, as far as the legal system was concerned, closed.

Reactions

The next day, the Supreme Court's decision in *Tinker v. Des Moines* was on the front page of newspapers such as the *New York Times* and, of course, the *Des Moines Register*. The story also appeared in the *Los Angeles Times*, but with the headline "Campus Rioters Warned by Court in D. M. Ruling," emphasizing that while the nonviolent, low-key armband protests in Des Moines might have been sanctioned by the Supreme Court, "protests causing 'substantial disorder or injuring the rights of others' would not be sanctioned."[11]

On February 26, 1969, the *New York Times* ran an editorial entitled "Armbands Yes, Miniskirts No":

> *In a fascinating decision Justice Fortas . . . said in effect that the Court is not going to worry about or interfere with disciplinary rules and*

trivia such as hair length, clean ears, blue jeans, or miniskirts. But the Court definitely intends to protect legitimate protest—by armband, button, or placard—as part of the general right to freedom of expression. . . . The . . . justices felt . . . a line could and should be drawn between free expression and disorderly excess.[12]

However, other newspaper editorials seemed to agree with Justice Black and his prediction that students were being given too much power and the educational system was going to suffer as a result. Richard Wilson, writing in the *Des Moines Register*, said, "The high court has sent tremors running through the educational system by its dictum that symbolic free speech may emerge from the mouths of babes at school. . . . The *Tinker* decision has seriously deranged higher education."[13]

The Students

How did those directly involved in the case react? Christopher, who was by that time attending college, responded that he was "overjoyed."[14] When asked if he had any comment on the more recent and more radical breed of student protests, he said he did not support violence and "that wasn't our case."[15] His father later wrote an article, responding in particular to Justice Black's assertion that the decision would bring a new era of permissiveness to the country. "Let's hope so!" William Eckhardt wrote. "Without permissiveness, democracy is a word without meaning."[16]

John, also in college, was surprised at first to hear of the decision, but later wrote a reaction to the case:

> *This decision has come at a time when many Americans are afraid of students. . . . It is ironic . . . that they should think that by claiming certain rights we were in some way destructive of the educational system. . . . If school systems cannot . . . provide students with the rights to which they are entitled, then they will be changed, and should be.*[17]

The events of the Vietnam War, and in particular the protests of students in college campuses, which were often violent and radical, had given some Americans a new fear of what students might do in society. Many people, as John noted, seemed to be afraid that allowing students the rights of free speech would destroy the educational system as they knew it.

> " What George [Washington] and the boys did for white males in 1776, what Abraham Lincoln did to a certain extent during the time of the Civil War for African-American males, what the women's suffrage movement in the 1920s did for women, the *Tinker* case did for children in America."[18]
>
> —*CHRISTOPHER ECKHARDT, 1999*

Mary Beth, still in high school at the time, was more personal in describing her response to the decision:

> *Suddenly it was mass hysteria. . . .* Time *magazine came and did this whole photo session at the school. They came to my chemistry class; it was really crazy. I was trying to make sense of it all. Where does this all fit in with my personal life? I was trying to make new friends and here I am, the maniac who's all over the news. All the kids were talking about it.*[19]

The court cases were over and the decision was made. But similar to most Supreme Court decisions, this one would have a lasting effect. And while the case would serve as a **precedent** in future cases, it would also be undermined by later rulings. ～

> By the time the Supreme Court decided our case in 1969, we had moved from Des Moines to St. Louis. . . . I was a junior in high school by then, sixteen years old. I was new in town, and I didn't know anyone. When you're that age, your friends are so important. I was like a fish out of water; I was kind of scared and shy. It was kind of a rough time when [the case was decided]. I was without as much personal support as when it happened, when I had a lot of my own friends around, and my parents' friends."[20]
>
> —MARY BETH TINKER

precedent—A ruling that serves as an example for future rulings on similar legal cases.

Chapter 10

After *Tinker*

ebruary 24, 1999, was the thirtieth anniversary of the *Tinker v. Des Moines* ruling. And although the case had never been overruled or even directly questioned in later rulings of the Supreme Court, it had not always been followed, either. As Erwin Chemerinsky wrote in "Students Do Leave Their First Amendment Rights at the Schoolhouse Gate: What's Left of *Tinker*?":

> Indeed the Supreme Court rulings subsequent to Tinker *have almost all sided with school officials and appear to have followed an approach much closer to Justice Black's than the majority.*[1]

Many free speech experts now fear students are steadily losing their right to free speech. *Tinker*

TINKER'S ANNIVERSARY

In 2009, marking the fortieth anniversary of the *Tinker* case, the Student Press Law Center's Executive Director Frank D. LoMonte wrote a guest column in the *Des Moines Register*:

> *Regrettably, it is hard to know whether to mark Tinker's anniversary with a birthday party or a [funeral]. Although Tinker remains the law of the land, reaffirmed as recently as 2007 by eight of nine Supreme Court justices, its protections have been hollowed out by later court rulings and the disregard of school administrators.*[2]

is considered a legal precedent, but it has not been expanded or successfully used in the Supreme Court to win another case since. The central ruling in the case, that students' First Amendment protection is determined by whether it causes a disruption, still stands and is applied to most related cases. However, no case following *Tinker* has had truly parallel circumstances. The ruling has remained fairly narrow in scope—that is, the *Tinker* students were protected by the First Amendment in their specific circumstances, but students in future cases with different circumstances might not be. Indeed, two cases concerning students' right to free speech that reached the Supreme Court since *Tinker* have potentially undermined the free speech gains made in the *Tinker* case.

Bethel School District No. 403 v. Fraser

In 1986, a case was brought before the Supreme Court concerning a student's speech at a school assembly. Matthew Fraser was a senior at Bethel High School in Pierce County, Washington, when he made a school council campaign speech on behalf of his friends at a school assembly. Almost 600 students, in grades 9 through 12, were at the assembly. Matthew's speech was not the usual campaign speech:

> *Fraser's speech included no profane or "dirty" words. But it was filled with sexually suggestive comments and gestures. Fraser's performance caused an uproar among many students in the audience, who hooted, cheered, laughed uproariously, and mimicked the sexual activities implied by the suggestive language. Many other members of the audience, however, appeared to be shocked and upset.*[3]

As a result of his speech, Matthew was suspended from school for three days and charged with violating the school's disorderly conduct rule. He was also told he would no longer be eligible to speak at his commencement ceremony. Matthew then protested that his First Amendment right to freedom of speech had been violated, and he sued the school district. The case

Matthew Fraser was suspended for making an inappropriate speech. The ruling in *Bethel v. Fraser* found that students have different rights to free speech than adults.

went to the Supreme Court in 1986. The Court voted against Matthew 7–2, and Justice Warren E. Burger wrote the court's opinion:

> It does not follow . . . that simply because the use of an offensive form of expression may not be prohibited to adults making what the speaker considers a political point, the same latitude must be permitted to children in a public school. The constitutional rights of students in public school are not automatically coextensive with the rights of adults in other settings.[4]

Justice Burger was saying students do not automatically have the same rights to free expression within their school that adults have in other places. The opinion continues:

> Surely it is a highly appropriate function of public school education to prohibit the use of vulgar and offensive terms in public discourse. . . . Nothing in the Constitution prohibits the states from insisting that certain modes of expression are inappropriate and subject to sanctions.[5]

Here Burger argues that certain types of expression in public schools—such as vulgar language—should be prohibited. He continues, saying it is the school board's job to decide what is or is not appropriate speech because schools are responsible for educating students in what is proper expression.

The court decided with this case that students in school do not automatically have the same constitutional

MORSE V. FREDERICK

In another famous Supreme Court case concerning student rights, *Morse v. Frederick*, principal Deborah Morse suspended Joseph Frederick from school in 2002 for displaying a sign that read "BONG HiTS 4 JESUS" at an Olympic torch parade in his town. The event took place off-campus and was not sponsored by the school, but it took place during school hours and the school had excused students from classes to attend. The court ruled in favor of the school, saying the principal did not violate Joseph's rights when she punished him for the banner, which he claimed was intended to be humorous. Critics claimed the Supreme Court was going back on its ruling in the *Tinker* case, since the event did not take place on school grounds and did not cause a disruption. As stated by the American Civil Liberties Union (ACLU),

> *The Court cannot have it both ways. Either this speech had nothing to do with drugs, which is what Joe Frederick claimed all along, or it was suppressed because school officials disagreed with the viewpoint it expressed on an issue that is very much the subject of debate . . . around the country.[6]*

rights as adults do outside of a school setting. This decision directly seemed to oppose the opinion written by Justice Fortas in the *Tinker* case, which proclaimed that students did not leave their constitutional rights at the door of the school. The decision also noted that the judicial system should take into account the authority and expertise of school officials. Justice Burger even finished

> The inculcation of these values is truly the 'work of the schools.' The determination of what manner of speech in the classroom or in school assembly is inappropriate properly rests with the school board. . . . The schools, as instruments of the state, may determine that the essential lessons of civil, mature conduct cannot be conveyed in a school that tolerates lewd, indecent, or offensive speech and conduct such as that indulged in by this confused boy."[7]
>
> —*JUSTICE BURGER, MAJORITY OPINION,*
> BETHEL V. FRASER

his written opinion with a quote from Justice Black's dissenting opinion in the *Tinker* case:

> *I wish therefore . . . to disclaim any purpose . . . to hold that the Federal Constitution compels the teachers, parents, and elected school officials to*

*surrender control of the American public school
system to public school students.*[8]

Hazelwood School District v. Kuhlmeier

A second case concerning students' rights to freedom
of speech surfaced in 1988 in Missouri. Students who
worked on their high school paper in a journalism
class protested when the high school's principal deleted
two pages of one issue of the newspaper. The pages
contained information about a student's pregnancy and
the use of birth control, as well as information about
another student's parents getting divorced. The principal
felt these pages were not appropriate for the readers
of the school paper. However, the student journalists,
including Cathy Kuhlmeier, claimed their rights to
freedom of expression were violated and sued Hazelwood
School District.

The Supreme Court decided against the students.
Justice Byron White wrote the court's majority opinion:

> *We have nonetheless recognized that the First
> Amendment rights of students in the public schools
> "are not automatically coextensive with the rights
> of adults in other settings," and must be "applied
> in light of the special characteristics of the school*

environment." . . . It is only when the decision to censor a school-sponsored publication, theatrical production, or other vehicle of student expression has no valid educational purpose that the First Amendment is so [involved] as to require judicial intervention to protect students' constitutional rights.[9]

The ruling in *Hazelwood v. Kuhlmeier* reinforced the ruling in the *Fraser* case, saying that the First Amendment rights of students in school were not the same as those of adults in other places.

There were also several cases involving students' Fourth Amendment rights, in which students protested schools' searches of student purses, backpacks, and lockers, as well as random drug testing. Again, the court ruled in favor of the schools, noting that school authorities needed to be able to maintain order. In these cases, the opinion of the Supreme Court majority in *Tinker* has largely been eclipsed by the dissenting opinion of Justice Black: that schools are institutions of authority and so the court will defer to the schools. As Professor Mark Yudof stated, "Although these [later decisions] have not specifically overruled *Tinker*, *Tinker*'s progeny have greatly altered the holding set forth by the Warren [Supreme] Court."[10]

However, experts note that *Bethel v. Fraser* and *Hazelwood v. Kuhlmeier* both concerned speech in situations that were not the same as *Tinker*. As Erwin Chemerinsky notes:

> In both [cases], the Court expressed concern that the school might be perceived as sponsoring or endorsing the speech. Tinker, *of course, did not concern this. It is appropriate to see* Bethel *and* Hazelwood, *in their specific holdings and*

STUDENT RIGHTS IN *NEW JERSEY V. T.L.O.*

Another famous Supreme Court case concerning student rights was *New Jersey v. T. L. O.* A student, known only by her initials, had her purse confiscated during school and searched. The resulting drug evidence was enough to bring state charges against her for delinquency. T. L. O. countered the charges with a request to suppress the evidence because her constitutional Fourth Amendment rights were violated with the unreasonable and unwarranted search and seizure of her purse. The court ruled against her in 1985, saying that in this instance, the school's search of her purse was reasonable and permissible. Again, the case showed that the court did not feel students automatically had the same constitutional rights in a school setting as adults did in another setting.

their general approach, as being limited to the public schools' ability to regulate speech in official programs and courses. Therefore, even in the light of Bethel *and* Hazelwood, *there remains First Amendment protection of student speech in non-curricular areas where there is no evidence of disruption of school activities.*[11]

In other words, *Tinker v. Des Moines* was different because wearing armbands did not disrupt the school, the speech was not part of an official school function or publication, and the question of inappropriate speech was not part of the case.

The Future of Students' Rights

Students' rights to free expression and free speech will continue to be high-profile issues, especially when it comes to situations such as student speeches and slogans on T-shirts and buttons, particularly those school administrators deem inappropriate. Many people feel there will be more instances of censorship as students have moved beyond relatively benign issues such as long hair and armbands to tougher issues including gang symbols, Satanic symbols, drugs, and body piercings. The courts will continue making decisions that

LIVES AFTER *TINKER*

Where were the three students from *Tinker v. Des Moines* in 2012?

- Mary Beth Tinker was a registered nurse with master's degrees in public health and nursing. She was actively involved in the Marshall-Brennan Constitutional Literacy project at American University and frequently spoke in schools about student rights.

- John Tinker was a computer consultant and also ran a project that donated used technology to Latin American countries. He was a conscientious objector during the Vietnam War and continued to be involved in antiwar, antinuclear, and environmental causes.

- Christopher Eckhardt was a consultant and writer. He was a conscientious objector during the Vietnam War, then he went on to work for the US Department of Justice as a mediator. He also worked as a reporter and for state correctional and social services and hosted his own public affairs television show.

distinguish whether schools are limiting student speech simply because it makes them uncomfortable or it is critical of school policies and personnel, or whether the schools are in situations in which they need to censor student speech to maintain authority. However, many free speech advocates feel censorship is becoming the norm. As Chemerinsky said in 2000, "Simply put, thirty years after *Tinker*, students do leave most of their First Amendment rights at the schoolhouse gate."[12] However, others see *Tinker* as a challenge and a reminder, such as legal scholar Jamin B. Raskin:

> Tinker *furnishes to us a provocative challenge and a standing invitation. It challenges us to make the promise of democratic freedom real in all of society's institutions . . . to actually carve out space . . . for citizens to speak and to hear one another, to engage in the unending and pervasive conversation that defines and constitutes political democracy.*[13]

> " I hope that if you have learned just one thing during our short time together it is that you as one person can make a difference, just as I did. It was one person after another that finally ended the Vietnam War."[14]
> —*CHRISTOPHER ECKHARDT SPEAKING TO STUDENTS, DECEMBER 3, 1991*

Raskin is saying if we are going to support the right of citizens to free speech, then we need to make sure we are allowing that free speech to take place, even in a school setting.

Mary Beth Tinker, who still visits schools to talk about her case and student rights, carries with her an even simpler message about *Tinker v. Des Moines* and

Mary Beth Tinker has become a free-speech activist.

subsequent court cases: "Teens, with their creativity, curiosity and (to some) outrageous sense of humor, are naturals when it comes to holding the First Amendment to the test of time."[15] She encourages the students she talks with to continue shaking things up. There will always be more cases that challenge student speech. Students themselves will always be in the best position to defend their own rights and, as legal scholar John W. Johnson said, "demand the right to be heard as well as seen."[16] ∼

Connecticut high school students protested their school's decision to ban Halloween costumes in 2007, defending their right to express themselves.

TIMELINE OF EVENTS
AND RULINGS

November — Members of the Tinker and Eckhardt families participate in a peace march in Washington DC.

December 11 — Students meet at the Eckhardt home to plan to protest the Vietnam War by wearing black armbands.

December 13 — The Roosevelt High School principal prevents publication of Ross Peterson's article about armbands.

December 14 — Des Moines area high school principals meet and decide to ban armbands from their schools.

December 16 — Christopher Eckhardt and Mary Beth Tinker wear black armbands to school and are suspended.

December 17 — John Tinker wears a black armband to school and is asked to leave. Two other students are suspended for wearing armbands.

December 21 — The Des Moines school board meets and votes to postpone a decision on armbands.

December 31 — The Des Moines school board conducts a secret meeting about the armband issue.

January 3 — The board votes to prohibit the wearing of armbands and uphold the suspension of students who did wear them.

1966	
January	Dan Johnston and the ICLU agree to represent the students in a lawsuit again the Des Moines school board.
July 25–26	*Tinker v. Des Moines* goes to trial before Judge Roy Stephenson in US district court.
September 1	Judge Stephenson upholds the school board's ban on the armbands.
1967	
April	*Tinker v. Des Moines* is heard in an appeals court, and the three-judge panel cannot come to a decision.
October	The case is heard again in front of an en banc panel of judges, who are equally divided. The lower court ruling stands.
1968	
March 4	The US Supreme Court agrees to hear *Tinker v. Des Moines*.
November 12	Lawyers present oral arguments to the US Supreme Court for *Tinker v. Des Moines*.
1969	
February 24	The Supreme Court announces its decisions in *Tinker v. Des Moines*. The court has voted 7–2 in favor of the students.

GLOSSARY

activist
> Someone who is especially active in working for or against a particular cause.

civil rights
> The rights of an individual to personal liberty and freedom, especially as established by the Thirteenth and Fourteenth Amendments to the US Constitution.

communism
> An economic system defined by collective ownership of property and the organization of labor for common advantage; a government system in which a single party holds power and the state controls the economy.

conservative
> Holding political views that tend to maintain tradition and existing conditions.

controversy
> A public disagreement or argument, especially concerning a matter of opinion.

counterculture
> The culture and lifestyle of people (especially young people) who reject or oppose the values of and behavior of society in general.

draft
> To take or select someone for military service.

incite

To stir up, provoke, or prompt an individual or group to take action.

liberal

Holding political views that tend to advocate increasing individual freedoms and civil liberties and changing government policy to advance these issues.

memorandum

An informal record or communication.

neo-Nazi

A modern group that agrees with the ideals of Adolf Hitler's German Nazi Party.

pacifist

A person who is strongly opposed to conflict and war.

parsonage

A church owned house provided for the pastor to live in.

picket

To demonstrate against the policies of a government or authority, usually by standing outside of a building or a meeting place.

segregation

The separation of a race, class, or ethnic group.

BRIEFS

Petitioners

John and Mary Beth Tinker and Christopher Eckhardt, and their fathers, Leonard Tinker and William Eckhardt, as "next friends" (because the students were minors)

Respondent

Des Moines Independent Community School District and several of its teachers, school board members, and administrators

Date of Ruling

February 24, 1969

Summary of Impacts

On December 16 and 17, 1965, students Christopher Eckhardt and Mary Beth and John Tinker wore black armbands to school to protest the Vietnam War and were suspended. Although the federal district court and the US court of appeals ruled against the students, the US Supreme Court ruled in their favor. One of the most important cases on the constitutional rights of students, *Tinker v. Des Moines* established that students have a right to free expression when it does not disrupt the educational purposes of the school or violate the rights of other students.

Quote

"First Amendment rights, applied in light of the special characteristics of the school environment, are available to teachers and students. It can hardly be argued that either students or teachers shed their constitutional rights to freedom of speech or expression at the schoolhouse gate."

—Justice Abe Fortas, in his majority opinion for the Supreme Court

ADDITIONAL RESOURCES

Selected Bibliography

Irons, Peter. *The Courage of Their Convictions: Sixteen Americans Who Fought Their Way to the Supreme Court*. New York: Penguin, 1990. Print.

Irons, Peter. *A People's History of the Supreme Court*. New York: Penguin, 2006. Print.

Johnson, John W. *The Struggle for Student Rights:* Tinker v. Des Moines *and the 1960s*. Lawrence, KS: U of Kansas P, 1997. Print.

Further Readings

Gold, Susan Dudley. *Supreme Court Milestones:* Tinker v. Des Moines: *Free Speech for Students*. New York: Benchmark Books, 2006. Print.

Hakim, Joy. *A History of Us: All the People 1945–1998*, Second Edition. New York: Oxford UP, 1999. Print.

Smith, Rich. *The First Amendment: The Right of Expression*. Minneapolis, MN: Abdo, 2007. Print.

Web Links

To learn more about *Tinker v. Des Moines*, visit ABDO Publishing Company online at **www.abdopublishing.com**. Web sites about *Tinker* are featured on our Book Links page. These links are routinely monitored and updated to provide the most current information available.

Places to Visit

The Newseum
555 Pennsylvania Avenue, NW
Washington, DC 20001
888-639-7386
http://www.newseum.org/index.html
The Newseum includes exhibits dedicated to the
First Amendment.

The Supreme Court of the United States
One First Street NE
Washington, DC 20543
202-479-3000
http://www.supremecourt.gov/
The Supreme Court building, home of the US judicial branch
of government, is located in Washington DC. Lectures,
exhibitions, and a film are available for visitors.

SOURCE NOTES

Chapter 1. The Right to Protest

1. David Hudson. "On 30-Year Anniversary, Tinker Participants Look Back at Landmark Case." *freedomforum.org*. Freedom Forum, 24 Feb. 1999. Web. 24 Apr. 2012.

2. Christopher Eckhardt. "*Tinker vs. Des Moines:* The True Story." *knol.google.com*. Google Knol, 13 Feb. 2011. Web. 24 Apr. 2012.

3. Henry David Thoreau. "Civil Disobedience—Part 2 of 3." *thoreau.eserver.org*. Thoreau Reader, n.d. Web. 1 May 2011.

4. "Interview Transcript with Mary Beth Tinker." *Civic Voices*. Civic Voices, 3 June 2010. PDF file. 24 Apr. 2012.

5. John W. Johnson. *The Struggle for Student Rights:* Tinker v. Des Moines *and the 1960s*. Lawrence, KS: U of Kansas P, 1997. Print. 27.

6. Ibid. 28.

7. "The Charters of Freedom: The Bill of Rights." *National Archives and Records Administration*. National Archives and Records Administration, n.d. Web. 24 Apr. 2012.

8. John W. Johnson. *The Struggle for Student Rights:* Tinker v. Des Moines *and the 1960s*. Lawrence, KS: U of Kansas P, 1997. Print. 28.

Chapter 2. 1965

1. Lyndon B. Johnson. "American Policy in Vietnam." *American Experience: Vietnam Online*. PBS Online/WGBH Boston, 7 Apr. 1965. Web. 24 Apr. 2012.

2. Doris Kearns Goodwin. *Lyndon Johnson and the American Dream*. New York: St. Martin's, 1991. 252. *Amazon.com Search*. Web. 24 Apr. 2012.

3. "Statistical Information about Casualties of the Vietnam War." *National Archives and Records Administration: Military Records*. National Archives and Records Administration, Feb. 2007. Web. 24 Apr. 2012.

4. Ibid.

5. Ibid.

6. Thomas Griffith. "Reagan's TV Troubles." *Time* 119.14 (5 Apr. 1982): 73. *EBSCO Academic Search Premier*. Web. 24 Apr. 2012.

7. Steven Laurence Danver. *Revolts, Protests, Demonstrations, and Rebellions in American History: An Encyclopedia*. Vol. 1. Santa Barbara, CA: ABC-CLIO, 2011. 931. *Google Book Search*. Web. 24 Apr. 2012.

Chapter 3. The Tinker and Eckhardt Families

1. "Friends Peace Testimony." *Quaker Information Center*. Quaker Information Center, 26 May 2011. Web. 24 Apr. 2012.

2. John W. Johnson. *The Struggle for Student Rights:* Tinker v. Des Moines *and the 1960s*. Lawrence, KS: U of Kansas P, 1997. Print. 14.

3. Ibid. 15.

4. Ibid. 13.

5. Ibid. 14.

6. Peter Irons. *The Courage of Their Convictions: Sixteen Americans Who Fought Their Way to the Supreme Court*. New York: Penguin, 1990. Print. 248.

7. John W. Johnson. *The Struggle for Student Rights:* Tinker v. Des Moines *and the 1960s*. Lawrence, KS: U of Kansas P, 1997. Print. 37.

8. Ibid. 31.

Chapter 4. The School Board Meets

1. John W. Johnson. *The Struggle for Student Rights:* Tinker v. Des Moines *and the 1960s*. Lawrence, KS: U of Kansas P, 1997. Print. 21.

2. Jack Magarrell. "D.M. Schools Ban Wearing of Viet Truce Armbands," *Des Moines Register* 15 Dec. 1965. 1. Quoted in Leigh Wolfe-Dawson. "A Biographical Study of Namesake John F. Tinker on the Landmark Legal Case *Tinker et al v. Des Moines Independent Community School District et al*." Diss. Colorado State U, 2008. *Google Book Search*. Web. 24 Apr. 2012.

3. John W. Johnson. *The Struggle for Student Rights:* Tinker v. Des Moines *and the 1960s*. Lawrence, KS: U of Kansas P, 1997. Print. 5.

4. Ibid. 22.

5. Ibid. 31.

6. Ibid. 30.

7. Ibid. 31.

8. Ibid. 32.

9. Ibid. 32.

10. Ibid. 32.

11. Ibid. 35.

12. Ibid. 34.

13. Peter Irons. *The Courage of Their Convictions: Sixteen Americans Who Fought Their Way to the Supreme Court.* New York: Penguin, 1990. Print. 236.

Chapter 5. The School Board Decides

1. John W. Johnson. *The Struggle for Student Rights:* Tinker v. Des Moines *and the 1960s.* Lawrence, KS: U of Kansas P, 1997. Print. 40.

2. Ibid. 38.

3. Ibid. 38.

4. Ibid. 39.

5. Ibid. 46.

6. Ibid. 59.

7. Ibid. 56.

Chapter 6. District Court Trial

1. 42 USC Sec. 1983. *Findlaw.* Findlaw, n.d. Web. 24 Apr. 2012.

2. John W. Johnson. *The Struggle for Student Rights:* Tinker v. Des Moines *and the 1960s.* Lawrence, KS: U of Kansas P, 1997. Print. 68.

3. Ibid. 69.

4. Ibid. 79.

5. Doreen Rappaport. *Be the Judge, BE the Jury:* Tinker vs. Des Moines: *Student Rights on Trial.* New York: Harper, 1993. Print. 39.

6. John W. Johnson. *The Struggle for Student Rights:* Tinker v. Des Moines *and the 1960s.* Lawrence, KS: U of Kansas P, 1997. Print. 97.

7. "The Charters of Freedom: The Constitution of the United States, Amendments 11–27." *National Archives and Records Administration.* National Archives and Records Administration, n.d. Web. 24 Apr. 2012.

8. Doreen Rappaport. *Be the Judge, BE the Jury:* Tinker vs. Des Moines: *Student Rights on Trial.* New York: Harper, 1993. Print. 74.

9. Tinker v. Des Moines Independent Community School Dist., 258 F. Supp. 971 (1966). US District Court S. D. Iowa. *Leagle.com.* Leagle, n.d. Web. 24 Apr. 2012.

10. Ibid.

11. Christopher Eckhardt. "1998 American Bar Association Online Conversations." Quoted in "Encyclopedia." *History of the*

Supreme Court. History of the Supreme Court, n.d. Web. 19 Mar. 2012.

    12. Tinker v. Des Moines Independent Community School Dist., 258 F. Supp. 971 (1966). US District Court S. D. Iowa. *Leagle. com.* Leagle, n.d. Web. 24 Apr. 2012.

Chapter 7. Court of Appeals Proceedings

    1. John W. Johnson. *The Struggle for Student Rights:* Tinker v. Des Moines *and the 1960s.* Lawrence, KS: U of Kansas P, 1997. Print. 105.

    2. Ibid. 118.

    3. "Rules of the Supreme Court of the United States." *US Supreme Court.* US Supreme Court, 12 Jan. 2010. PDF file. 24 Apr. 2012.

    4. John W. Johnson. *The Struggle for Student Rights:* Tinker v. Des Moines *and the 1960s.* Lawrence, KS: U of Kansas P, 1997. Print. 123.

Chapter 8. The Supreme Court Hears the Case

    1. Patricia Sullivan. "General Commanded Troops in Vietnam." *Washington Post.* Washington Post, 19 July 2005. Web. 24 Apr. 2012.

    2. John W. Johnson. *The Struggle for Student Rights:* Tinker v. Des Moines *and the 1960s.* Lawrence, KS: U of Kansas P, 1997. Print. 143.

    3. Ibid. 146.

    4. Peter Irons. *The Courage of Their Convictions: Sixteen Americans Who Fought Their Way to the Supreme Court.* New York: Penguin, 1990. Print. 241.

    5. John W. Johnson. *The Struggle for Student Rights:* Tinker v. Des Moines *and the 1960s.* Lawrence, KS: U of Kansas P, 1997. Print. 157.

    6. "Tinker v. Des Moines Ind. Comm. School Dist.: Oral Argument Transcript." *The Oyez Project.* IIT Chicago-Kent College of Law, n.d. Web. 24 Apr. 2012.

    7. David L. Hudson Jr. "On 30-Year Anniversary, *Tinker* Participants Look Back at Landmark Case." *First Amendment Center.* First Amendment Center, 24 Feb. 1999. Web. 24 Apr. 2012.

    8. John W. Johnson. *The Struggle for Student Rights:* Tinker v. Des Moines *and the 1960s.* Lawrence, KS: U of Kansas P, 1997. Print. 158.

    9. Peter Irons. *The Courage of Their Convictions: Sixteen Americans Who Fought Their Way to the Supreme Court.* New York: Penguin, 1990. Print. 240–241.

10. John W. Johnson. *The Struggle for Student Rights:* Tinker v. Des Moines *and the 1960s.* Lawrence, KS: U of Kansas P, 1997. Print. 166.

Chapter 9. The Decision

1. Patricia Sullivan. "General Commanded Troops in Vietnam." *Washington Post.* Washington Post, 19 July 2005. Web. 24 Apr. 2012.

2. "TINKER v. DES MOINES SCHOOL DIST., 393 US 503 (1969)." FindLaw. FindLaw, n. d. Web. 24 Apr. 2012.

3. Ibid.

4. Ibid.

5. Ibid.

6. Ibid.

7. John W. Johnson. *The Struggle for Student Rights:* Tinker v. Des Moines *and the 1960s.* Lawrence, KS: U of Kansas P, 1997. Print. 170–171.

8. "TINKER v. DES MOINES SCHOOL DIST., 393 US 503 (1969)." FindLaw. FindLaw, n. d. Web. 24 Apr. 2012.

9. Ibid.

10. Ibid.

11. John W. Johnson. *The Struggle for Student Rights:* Tinker v. Des Moines *and the 1960s.* Lawrence, KS: U of Kansas P, 1997. Print. 181.

12. "Armbands Yes, Miniskirts No," *New York Times*, 26 Feb. 1969. Quoted in Leigh Wolfe-Dawson. "A Biographical Study of Namesake John F. Tinker on the Landmark Legal Case *Tinker et al v. Des Moines Independent Community School District et al.*" Diss. Colorado State U, 2008. *Google Book Search*. Web. 24 Apr. 2012.

13. John W. Johnson. *The Struggle for Student Rights:* Tinker v. Des Moines *and the 1960s.* Lawrence, KS: U of Kansas P, 1997. Print. 182.

14. Ibid. 183.

15. Ibid. 183.

16. Ibid. 183.

17. Ibid. 183–184.

18. David L. Hudson Jr. "On 30-Year Anniversary, *Tinker* Participants Look Back at Landmark Case." *First Amendment Center.* First Amendment Center, 24 Feb. 1999. Web. 24 Apr. 2012.

19. Peter Irons. *The Courage of Their Convictions: Sixteen Americans Who Fought Their Way to the Supreme Court*. New York: Penguin, 1990. Print. 249.

20. Ibid. 249.

Chapter 10. After *Tinker*

1. Erwin Chemerinsky. "Students Do Leave Their First Amendment Rights at the Schoolhouse Gate: What's Left of *Tinker?*" *Drake Law Review* 48 (2000): 535. Print.

2. Mark Walsh. "Tinker v. Des Moines at 40," *Education Week*. Editorial Projects in Education, 24 Feb. 2009. Web. 24 Apr. 2012.

3. John J. Patrick. *The Supreme Court of the United States: A Student Companion*. 2nd ed. New York: Oxford UP, 2001. Print. 37.

4. "BETHEL SCHOOL DIST. NO. 403 v. FRASER, 478 US 675 (1986)." FindLaw. FindLaw, n. d. Web. 24 Apr. 2012.

5. Ibid.

6. "ACLU Slams Supreme Court Decision in Student Free Speech Case." *American Civil Liberties Union.* American Civil Liberties Union, 25 June 2007. Web. 24 Apr. 2012.

7. "BETHEL SCHOOL DIST. NO. 403 v. FRASER, 478 US 675 (1986)." FindLaw. FindLaw, n. d. Web. 24 Apr. 2012.

8. Erwin Chemerinsky. "Students Do Leave Their First Amendment Rights at the Schoolhouse Gate: What's Left of *Tinker?*" *Drake Law Review* 48 (2000): 537. Print.

9. "HAZELWOOD SCHOOL DISTRICT v. KUHLMEIER, 484 US 260 (1988)." FindLaw. FindLaw, n. d. Web. 24 Apr. 2012.

10. Erwin Chemerinsky. "Students Do Leave Their First Amendment Rights at the Schoolhouse Gate: What's Left of *Tinker?*" *Drake Law Review* 48 (2000): 541. Print.

11. Ibid. 542.

12. Ibid. 546.

13. Jamin B. Raskin, "No Enclaves of Totalitarianism: The Triumph and Unrealized Promise of the Tinker Decision." *American University Law Review* 58 (2009): 1220. Print.

14. Christopher Eckhardt. "The Day I Wore a Black Armband to School." Speech to students in Boston, December 3, 1991. *Rightsmatter.org*. Bill of Rights Network, 1991. Web. 24 Apr. 2012.

SOURCE NOTES CONTINUED

15. "Tinker v. Des Moines (393 U.S. 503, 1969)." *American Civil Liberties Union*. American Civil Liberties Union, 16 Mar. 2007. Web. 24 Apr. 2012.

16. John W. Johnson. *The Struggle for Student Rights:* Tinker v. Des Moines *and the 1960s*. Lawrence, KS: U of Kansas P, 1997. Print. 217.

INDEX

A

American Civil Liberties Union, 17, 18, 129

American Friends Service Committee, 41, 62

B

Bethel v. Fraser, 126–130

Black, Hugo, 100, 101, 102

Black Like Me, 38–39

Blackman, Donald, 81–82

Brennan, William J., Jr., 100, 135

Burger, Warren E., 128, 130

Burnside v. Byars, 92–93

C

Caudill, George, 55, 57

China, 22, 23, 44

civil disobedience, 12, 13

civil rights, 13, 17, 20, 30, 34, 38–39, 40, 43, 45

protests, 33, 39, 46

Clark, Bruce, 12–13

communism, 9, 10, 22–23, 34, 47

constitutional amendments, 74

First, 18, 34, 71, 73, 81, 82–83, 102, 107, 111, 114, 124–125, 126, 131–132, 134, 135, 138

Fourth, 132, 133

Fourteenth, 73, 81, 83, 107, 114

Fifteenth, 31

D

Davis, Arthur, 55

Davis, Dwight, 18

Democratic Party, 22

Des Moines School District School Board, 12, 14, 17, 18–19, 53–57, 58, 60, 63–64, 66–67, 69, 70, 73, 82, 103–104

Douglas, William O., 100, 102, 107

draft system, 23–25

INDEX CONTINUED

About the Author

Marcia Amidon Lusted is the author of more than 60 nonfiction books for young readers, as well as hundreds of magazine articles. She is an assistant editor for Cobblestone Publishing's six magazines for children, as well as a writing instructor and musician. She lives in New Hampshire.

About the Content Consultant

Gerald Thain is professor of law emeritus at the University of Wisconsin–Madison. His expertise includes advertising law and the First Amendment.